TALKING
AND LEARNING

The Lakatos Primary Mathematics Group

George Ball
Elizabeth Davies
Pamela Eyles
Denise Thomas
Margaret Wagner

TALKING AND LEARNING

Primary Maths for
the National Curriculum

GEORGE BALL

with the

LAKATOS PRIMARY MATHEMATICS GROUP

SIMON & SCHUSTER
EDUCATION

© George Ball 1990

First published in 1990 by
Basil Blackwell Ltd

Reprinted in 1992 by
Simon & Schuster Education

Simon & Schuster Education
Campus 400
Maylands Avenue
Hemel Hempstead
Herts HP2 7EZ

All rights reserved. No part of this publication may be reproduced, stored in a retrieval system, or transmitted in any form or by any means, electronic, mechanical, photocopying, recording or otherwise, without the prior permission of Simon & Schuster Education.

Although the whole of this book remains subject to copyright, permission is granted to photocopy pages 40–44 and 55–122 for distribution and use only in the school which has purchased the book.

British Library Cataloguing in Publication Data
Ball, George
  Talking and learning.
  1. Mathematics
  I. Title II. Lakatos Primary Mathematics Group
  510

ISBN 0-7501-0430-9

Printed in Great Britain by Dotesios Ltd, Trowbridge

Contents

Preface	vi
Acknowledgements	viii

Part One   Discussion-based Teaching

1	Why is Mathematical Discussion Important?	3
2	What is Meant by Discussion?	9
3	Getting Started	14
4	Evaluating Discussion Activities	22
5	Planning and Organising Discussion	28
6	Sharing Ideas – Some Inset Activities	38

Part Two   A Resource Pack for Developing a Discussion-based Approach

7	Handling Mathematical Discussion – A Summary of Key Ideas	47
8	Discussion Activities	53

Number	55
Algebra	74
Measures	87
Shape and Space	93
Handling Data	108

Bibliography	123
Index	124

Preface

There is much emphasis within the National Curriculum on children being able to use and apply the mathematics they are learning. It is recognised that it is important for children to be able to talk about their own ideas, describing and explaining their current thinking as well as making and testing predictions based on personal experience. This requires that the children clearly understand the mathematics that they do. Mechanical manipulation of numbers and symbols, even when it produces a 'correct' answer, can no longer be considered sufficient; there must also be the opportunity for children to discuss and reflect upon their experiences so that they are able to 'make sense' of the mathematics they meet. Consequently, the teacher needs to plan for groups of children to come together to share and compare their ideas and perceptions. During these sessions it is the teacher's job to exploit and refine the ideas offered by the children so that they are able to negotiate a fuller understanding of the underlying mathematics. This style of teaching is termed 'discussion-based' and requires a different set of teaching skills and organisational strategies than the more familiar and traditional didactic approach. It is the purpose of this book to provide practical help for teachers who want to develop a discussion-based approach in their own classrooms.

The book is in two parts. Part One (pages 1–44) considers why discussion is important, how the approach differs from conventional question and answer sessions, and what advantages are offered. There is advice on how to begin to implement the teaching style, ideas for evaluating discussion sessions, and suggestions to help with organisation and planning. The advice and suggestions are supported by a series of case studies which serve to illustrate the ideas put forward.

Each section ends with a series of teacher activities which can be used on an individual or a group basis. The activities are designed to provide the reader with some practical experience of discussion-based teaching, and a fuller understanding of this approach. There is also a section dealing with Inset activities which should act as a useful resource for advisory teachers, mathematics coordinators, or Inset providers who wish to encourage staff development in this important area.

The second part of the book (pages 45–122) is a resource pack of ideas and activities for teachers to use in their own classrooms. Many of these activities may already be familiar, but they are presented and developed in a way which places emphasis on the discussion-based approach. Indeed, many of these include case study material which has been linked back to the key ideas presented in the first part of the book and summarised at the beginning of the second.

The activities themselves are presented under the National Curriculum topic headings of Number, Algebra, Measures, Shape and Space, and Handling Data, and are referenced to the appropriate attainment targets. However, as mathematics is interrelated and is not made up of discrete units, it is important to realise that activities listed in any one section will undoubtedly influence and broaden children's experiences of other topics. For example, a sorting activity, nominally identified as being Shape and Space (Attainment Target 10) may well provide opportunities for number work, pattern identification, comparative use of measures, and/or data collection.

Again, although the case study material describes work carried out with lower primary age children, many of the activities lend themselves to work with older primary children. This is certainly true of the overall philosophy which is not tied to any particular age or ability band, and is an appropriate part of any balanced approach to teaching.

Acknowledgements

Grateful thanks are extended to Tom Brissenden who, as a founder member of the Lakatos Primary Mathematics Group, provided us with the enthusiasm and opportunity to produce this book. Many of the ideas discussed here are developed further in a companion book by Tom Brissenden with the Lakatos Primary Mathematics Group, *Talking about Mathematics* (Basil Blackwell, 1988).

Thanks are also due to Suzanne Ball for her support and hard work while preparing the manuscript, and to Janet Wyn George for her help in developing case study material for 'Across the River' and 'Jumping Beans'.

Part One

DISCUSSION-BASED TEACHING

1 Why is Mathematical Discussion Important?

Language and discussion are essential parts of the learning process. Since the 1960s the work of Piaget has provided much of the theoretical basis for our primary mathematics teaching and has resulted in great emphasis being placed on the role of practical work in the classroom. Although no one would dispute the importance of such practical experience, Piaget placed little significance on the part played by the child's interaction with people. In recent years research has suggested that such interactions, which allow the sharing and comparing of one another's ideas and perceptions, have an important part to play in the development of understanding and the child's ability to grasp meaning. The ability to 'negotiate meaning', or to 'make sense of things', appears to us to be of paramount importance, and is vital if children are to use and apply mathematics in the manner advocated within the National Curriculum. This view has resulted in the notion of the child as a 'mathematical thinker' who needs to be given more responsibility and opportunity to develop his/her own learning. Consequently, we believe that it is important for children to come together to talk about the mathematics that they are doing. As well as helping children to 'negotiate meaning', such discussion-based activity can also provide additional advantages, as we shall now see.

Improving language, social and personal skills

Consider the following activity in which four reception class children are scattering small cubes on to sheets of plain paper. Each child has five cubes which are held in a cupped hand and rolled, in one movement, on to an individual piece of paper. In the extract below the four children and their teacher are discussing the resulting patterns which are shown in Figure 1.1.

4 Discussion-based teaching

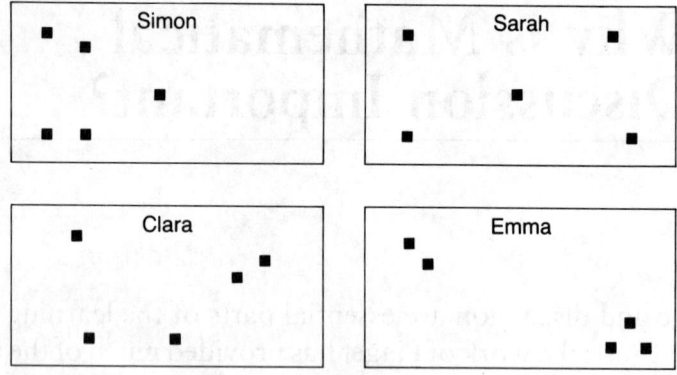

Figure 1.1

Simon: I see a set of 2 and 2 and 1.
Sarah: A set of 1 and 1 and 1 and 1 and 1.
Clara: 1 and 2 and 1 and 1.
Emma: A set of 2 and 1 and 1 and 1. Miss, that's 5 altogether.
Simon: Miss, I got 5 altogether. I got 2 and another 1 is 3, and another 1 is 4, and another 1 is 5. 5 altogether.
Emma: Miss, Simon had 2, and another 2 is 4, and 1 more is 5.
Teacher: Sarah, how many do you have altogether?
Sarah: Miss, five 'loads' of ones.
Teacher: How many sets of 1?
Sarah: Five ones.
Clara: Miss, I've got 5 altogether as well.
Emma: We've all got 5, but different.
Teacher: Can you explain what you mean to us, Emma?
Emma: Well, Miss, Simon had 2 and 2 and 1, and Sarah had 1 and 1 and 1 and 1 and 1, and I had 3 and 2. They all make fives but different sets, Miss.
Teacher: Good girl, Emma. They all make 5 but in different ways. Have you made the same sets as Clara?
Emma: Um, no.
Teacher: Well, how are they different?
Emma: I can see 2 first, then 1 and 1 and 1.
Teacher: What about you, Clara?
Clara: Well, Miss, I got 1 first then 2 and 1 and 1.
Emma: See, Miss, same sets but different pattern. Different way, isn't it, Miss?
Teacher: Good. What other sets might we have made?
Sarah: Miss, um, 4 and ...
Simon: Miss, 4 and a one-set. That will make 5. [*Simon physically separates the cubes to illustrate his idea.*]

Teacher: Are there any other sets we might have made?
Emma: A set of 2 and a set of 3; that will make 5. [*Emma also moves her cubes to arrive at this result.*]

An obvious advantage of introducing more talk into our mathematics lessons is the opportunity it provides for improving general language skills. In the above example the children are being encouraged to develop their communicative skills by articulating ideas clearly, listening to one another and using appropriate language (notice how the teacher reacts to Sarah's use of 'loads', by injecting the correct terminology 'sets' back into the discussion). Related to this are advantages in terms of promoting group, social and personal skills. Mathematics appears to have contributed little or nothing to this aspect of the school curriculum, where other subjects such as English predominate. Yet the potential is obviously considerable – learning to work as a member of a group, taking turns, expressing ideas, acting as spokesperson, giving and receiving criticism, arguing for and against in a logical way, and so on.

Sharing ideas leads to better understanding

More importantly from the mathematical standpoint is the fact that opportunities to discuss, share and compare ideas will result in a better understanding of the underlying concepts. Children have varying perceptions of the world in which we live. These perceptions differ from child to child and will undoubtedly differ from those of the teacher. There is a great danger in failing to recognise this and in assuming that children see things in the same way as we do. This can result in a breakdown of communications, with children interpreting instructions and questions in quite a different way than was intended. By adopting a more discussion-based approach we minimise this 'mismatch' and allow children to negotiate a fuller meaning from the experiences we provide. In this respect the understanding gained from the activity described above should reveal itself in later investigative work when the children are more mature and better able to handle systematic recording of results. Indeed, when the same group of children repeated the activity using six cubes, their previous experience was clearly evident. After preliminary statements relating to the patterns thrown –

Simon: A set of 1 and 2 and 1 and 1 and 1. [*6 = 1 + 2 + 1 + 1 + 1.*]

Emma: I can see a set of 2 and 1 and 1 and 1 and 1. [6 = 2 + 1 + 1 + 1 + 1.] Four lots of 1 and a 2, that's six altogether! [4 × 1 + 2 = 6.]
Clara: I can see a set of 3 and a 2 and a set of 1. [6 = 3 + 2 + 1.]
Sarah: Miss, 4 and a set of 2 makes 6. [4 + 2 = 6.]

– the children were all keen to experiment by moving their cubes around in a search for further results:

Emma: 5 and 1 more makes 6.
Clara: 3 and 3 makes 6.
Simon: 4 and 2 makes 6.
Sarah: Miss, here's a set of 6, and that makes 6!

Promoting positive attitudes towards maths

A further advantage of this approach lies in the opportunities that it provides for promoting positive attitudes towards mathematics. This is an important consideration and efforts should be made to make the children feel comfortable and 'at home' with mathematics. By demonstrating that we value the contribution that each child is able to make we help to develop self-esteem and encourage positive attitudes.

Assessment

Finally there are the assessment opportunities that this type of work offers. Observing and listening to children during discussion provides the teacher with a continuous and detailed means of assessing individual understanding and progress. During discussion it is possible to identify problems and misconceptions and respond appropriately and flexibly on the spot. As a diagnostic tool, discussion is far more effective than any other mode of assessment.

The assessment opportunities that discussion provides are recognised within the National Curriculum. The standard assessment tasks at age 7 will rely largely upon activity-based approaches that centre around extended pieces of work which are 'open' in nature (that is, tasks that allow pupils to have some control over the direction they take and the methods they use) and which are undertaken on a group basis. It is envisaged that these tasks, along with the resulting discussion, will then be used to assess each child's knowledge, skills, understanding, initiative, planning, and team work.

Returning to the above example, we see that the task set was 'open'. The children were active and contributed to the development of the session. Even in the short report given, there are obvious opportunities for assessment – all the children work well together; they are all willing to contribute; Emma appears to have a sound understanding of the conservation (or 'sameness') of 5, while Simon shows initiative in rearranging his cubes to produce a new number statement.

This type of activity can be easily extended. Clara, Emma, Sarah and Simon went on to repeat the activity with six cubes, while a further possibility might be an investigation of the number bonds of 5 using Multilink or Cuisenaire rods. Such an investigation is not as straightforward as it may at first appear (how many number combinations can you find?) and you should not expect young children to identify all possibilities. Nevertheless, the structured nature of the apparatus should encourage the children to be more systematic than they might otherwise have been, as well as providing a semi-permanent means of recording the children's work.

The recording of results is an important step in the search for new relationships. It allows the children to keep track of their discoveries and helps them to predict further possibilities. During the cube-rolling activity the position of the cubes themselves provides both the opportunity for the discovery (and statement) of a number bond, and the means of recording it. Writing a number sentence would have been inappropriate, and although moving the cubes allows the children to discover further results, it also means that the original ones are lost. Using apparatus such as Multilink or Cuisenaire means that a whole series of results can be built up, compared and displayed. At the end of the activity, if a more permanent record of the group's work is required, the children could copy their arrangements onto squared paper and colour them.

A permanent record of the cube-rolling activity could be achieved by gluing the cubes (or some buttons or counters) onto stiff card to produce a collage. This could then be displayed for children and parents as evidence of work completed. However, in either case it is the *doing* and the *talking* that are of greatest value, and while recording is often very necessary, it should not be seen as the sole purpose or outcome of any activity.

Summary

In this chapter we have outlined our reasons for believing discussion to be an important part of the learning process. Introducing more

8 *Discussion-based teaching*

'talk' into our mathematics teaching can produce benefits in a variety of ways as indicated in Figure 1.2. In addition, discussion provides opportunities to assess, diagnose, and respond to children's strengths and weaknesses flexibly and on the spot.

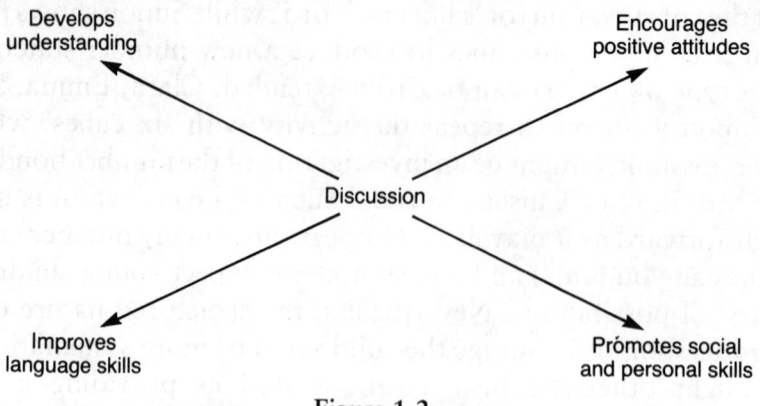

Figure 1.2

Teacher activities

1.1 Try to recall some recent conversations you may have had with pupils during a mathematics lesson. What did these conversations tell you about the children concerned? Next time you talk to children about mathematics try and consider their responses in terms of the four categories described above.

1.2 How would you find the difference between 47 and 79? Ask your colleagues and friends how they might tackle the same problem. Encourage them to explain exactly what method they use. For example, did they count on to 50 and add 29? Or did they perhaps count on to 49 and add 30? See how many different methods you can identify.

What about the difference between 22 and 45, or the difference between 69 and 87? Did each person use the same method each time? Did different people have similar approaches?

2 What is Meant by Discussion?

Discussion means something more than the short question-and-answer routines which often arise during traditional class or group teaching. In such a form of questioning the teacher has a good idea of what makes a reasonable answer – the teacher's 'ideal response' – and the questions themselves are intended to allow the children to arrive at a particular answer. The nature of the questions is termed 'closed' and there is the constant temptation on the teacher's part to match the pupils' answers with the 'ideal response' by commenting on everything that is offered. These comments usually take the form of an evaluation which makes it clear to the class whether an answer is accepted as 'right' or 'wrong'. A clear pattern emerges.

Teacher asks question
(with an 'ideal response' in mind)
↓
Pupil responds
↓
Teacher comments
(matching the pupil's reply with the 'ideal response',
so as to accept or reject it)

Even though a number of children may be involved, little or no discussion occurs. The pupils speak to the teacher, not to one another. Although the children may listen to the teacher, they do not necessarily pay close attention to each other's comments.

Encouraging children to make mathematical statements

In discussion, people listen to one another and have the opportunity to contribute freely – there is *not* someone who evaluates and comments on everything that is said. If we are to introduce discussion into our mathematics teaching then activities and questions which encourage children to share and compare their ideas are necessary. Consider the following example in which six reception class children are using sorting trays and a collection of colourful plastic objects. Each child has a tray and a card showing a numeral.

Teacher: Look at the number in the middle of your tray and tell me what it says. Can you make sets of that number in your tray?

The children have had some experience of making sets previously and are all able to identify and *make a statement* concerning their particular number.

Gavin: Miss, I've got a 4.
Ceri: I've got a 5 so I've got to use lots of things.

Note the opportunity for each child to speak and the resulting advantages in terms of language development (pay attention to articulation and make sure all the other children are listening carefully to the child speaking), social awareness ('taking turns' is important), and assessment opportunities.

Once each child had contributed orally, the sorting activity progressed with little further talk. When all the children appeared to have completed their sets the teacher drew the group back together.

Teacher: Let's all have a look at the sets we have been making in our trays. Simon, tell us what you have done.

Opening up the situation

The intention now is to get more 'talk' going as each child is given the opportunity to report on what he/she has done.

The teacher then 'opens up' the situation by challenging the children to *change* the number of objects in their sorting trays. This, in our experience, produces some interesting developments.

Teacher: Now, Sarah, how are you going to change your set [*of 4*] to make a set of 3?
Sarah: 1 and 1 and 1 is 3 [*holding up her fingers*]. I'll take 1 out.
Teacher: Does everyone agree? Has anyone got another way of doing it?

Notice that teacher does not merely accept Sarah's statement as being correct. She wants the other children to be involved and to take that decision for themselves. She also wants to draw out any other methods the children may have so that they can be shared and discussed. This is an important strategy and one that is worth developing. Try not to evaluate openly the children's contributions before *they* have had the opportunity to consider and discuss them.

Kelly [*working with her set of 4*]: Miss, 1 and 1 and 1 is 3 [*moving the objects in the tray and speaking at the same time*] so I can take 1 out and I've got 3 left.
Teacher: Simon, what sets have you made?
Simon: Sets of 3.
Teacher: Can you make a new set with this number [5]?
Simon: 1 and 1 and 1 and 1 and 1 is 5 [*holding up each finger on his left hand as he chants, then comparing with three fingers held up on his right hand*] ... I need two more in each bit [*right hand and set?*] to make 5!
Teacher: Does everyone agree? Well done. Simon had 3 and he will need 2 more to make 5. *Three add two makes five.*

Notice here how the teacher recapped and then presented the children with the language pattern she eventually wanted them to use. 'Three add two makes five.'

We see more evidence of this when Gavin was challenged to change his set of 5 into a set of 1.

Gavin: I've got to take 1, 2, 3, 4 out [*physically touching objects*]. Miss, 4 and 1 makes 5 altogether. It's like Simon, Miss. 1 and 4 makes 5 and Simon says 3 and 2 makes 5.

It is particularly interesting to note how Gavin used the commutative result 4 + 1 = 1 + 4 in this last statement, and how he was able to relate it back to Simon's earlier experience of making a set of 5.

A further interesting development occurred when Ceri attempted to make a set of 3 from an existing set of 5 and introduced a language pattern which would normally be associated with subtraction.

Ceri: Miss, I must take some out. I must take out 3 to make a set of 3 ... Oh no, that's too many. Only 2 ... yes, that's right. *I had 5, take away 2, that makes 3.*

Summary

In this chapter we have identified the essential features of a discussion-based approach by reference to a particular classroom episode. Notice that:

- The activity around which the discussion centres is a common one which is familiar to most primary teachers.
  Such an activity can often progress on an individual or group basis without any useful discussion.
- Opportunities for talk can be introduced by requiring each child to make initial statements about the nature of the task. This in itself will be valuable in developing language and social skills, assessing understanding, and diagnosing problems.

  The strategy of requiring each child in turn (varying the starting position) to talk about his/her perception of the problem in hand is an important and recurring one. In the above example the teacher encouraged each child to describe and compare the sets they had made and then moved on to issue further challenges.
- By presenting a new challenge (requiring the child to change the number of objects in her/his tray), the situation is 'opened up' to allow the children to develop their own thinking and use of language.

  The new challenge can be matched to the perceived needs of the child. For example, Gavin seems to be coping well and is challenged to make a set of 5 into a set of 1; Sarah, who was identified as having some difficulty (not reported here), is asked to change her set of 4 into a set of 3.

  Each child articulates the required change to the group and not just to the teacher. The teacher accepts what is offered and seeks to involve the other children before commenting. Phrases such as 'Does everyone agree?' and 'What do you think, Simon?' are useful in this respect.
- Further activities should be planned in order to consolidate and/or enhance the ideas that the children encounter. In the present example, modifications and/or extensions might include the cube-rolling, Multilink or Cuisenaire activities outlined in Chapter 1, or the pattern work described in Chapter 3.

Teacher activities

2.1 Consider the various ways in which we use language. For example, we might use language to ask a question, give an order, or offer advice. Draw up a list of as many usages as you can. Consider when and how you use these various forms in the classroom.

2.2 Next time you are working with children, try to avoid asking 'closed' questions – that is, questions which are designed to allow children to arrive at your 'ideal response'. Instead, ask 'open' questions which allow the children to answer in their own way and from their own starting point.

Some examples of 'open' questions are:

- Can you tell/show us what you have been doing?
- What do you think might happen if ... ?
- What do you expect will happen?
- Will it work if ... ?
- Can you tell us what you mean?

When a child responds, try not to evaluate or comment on the answer except to involve *other* children in the discussion. Suitable questions to ask at this stage might be:

- Does anyone else have a different idea/method/view?
- What do *you* (a different child) think?
- How can we check that?

3 Getting started

Discussion is a teaching style which is best suited to some form of classroom organisation which involves group work. True discussion is very difficult when class teaching predominates, or when children work almost exclusively in an individualised way from commercial schemes. The following advice is offered to teachers who wish to begin developing their experience of discussion work.

- Choose a group of four to six children that you feel you would like to work with.
- Plan a short activity that appeals to you and which you feel is appropriate for the children.

    You might like to use an activity from your school scheme or one of those outlined in this book. In some instances we have included considerable detail concerning the development of an activity. Beware of attempting to reproduce an identical session. Remember that the children should have some control over the proceedings and that you need to respond to their ideas. By being aware of possibilities that may present themselves, you should be able to exploit these ideas more fully than might otherwise have been the case.
- Settle the rest of the class and make sure that they are profitably occupied with work which will not demand your immediate attention.
- Arrange your group so that they are facing one another. Sit with them and make it clear that you want them to talk.
- Introduce the activity to the children and then, *before they begin the activity*, encourage each child in turn to tell the group what they think has to be done.

You may well be surprised by the range of answers and the diversity of their interpretations! At some time or other most of us have experienced a breakdown of communications. In the classroom this can be a particularly frustrating and perplexing experience as the teacher 'directs' children in certain activities only to find that the instructions are apparently ignored or misinterpreted. In such circumstances it can appear as though the teacher is speaking in a foreign language which the children are unable to fully comprehend; there is a 'mismatch' between the teacher's perception of the problem and that of the child. The initial sharing of ideas should help the group to negotiate some common understanding of what is (or should be!) required. This can be very instructive for the teacher who may find that the situation holds far more possibilities than she/he had previously realised! (Be flexible and prepared to go along with the children's ideas.) It also provides an immediate opportunity for each child to speak and listen to one another, thus giving the teacher an early indication of any problems individual children are likely to have.

The same strategy of asking each child what they have to do, what they are doing, or what they have done can be incorporated at various stages in any activity, and provides the teacher with a means of finding out more about each child's thinking. When using this strategy repeatedly, make sure that you start with a different child each time so that everyone takes a turn speaking first.

An alternative way of giving a group a common purpose is by providing them with a piece of apparatus or worksheet, and allowing the children themselves to decide what they should do with it. In the example below, four top infants were presented with copies of the worksheet shown in Figure 3.1. (The letters shown are for reference purposes only and did not appear on the original.)

Teacher: Can anyone guess what I am going to ask you to do? [*No response.*] Well, look at the number 10 in the middle of the paper. It's an answer ... an answer to what? [*Silence as the children all peer anxiously at their papers.*] Here's a clue then ... look up the row from the 10.
Lisa: There's a 4.
Teacher: That's right. Now look across the row from the 10.
Lisa: 6 [*Pause.*] ... It's 6 add 4 equals 10.
Teacher: How do you know that it's 6 add 4, Lisa?
Lisa: 'Cos that makes 10.
Rachel: But it says 'add' in the corner. ... I think I've got the idea now, Miss. This one [*pointing to square* a] is 5 because 2 add 3 makes 5.
Teacher: Can you explain why you are adding 2 and 3?
Rachel: You have to look up and look across so it is 2 add 3.
Lisa: It's easy now.
Teacher: What should we put in this square, Liam [e]?

16 *Discussion-based teaching*

Liam [*After a pause*]: That's 6 add 2.
Rachel [*Interrupting*]: Up the top of the square first – it's 2 add 6.
Liam: Oh yes. [*Counts on his fingers*] So it's 8.
Teacher: Good. What about this square [b], Owain?
Owain: Um! Is it 4 add 3?
Teacher: Right, so what should go in the square?
Owain: 7.
Teacher: Good boy. I think you can all finish filling in your worksheets now.

+	2	4	8	0
3	a	b	c	d
6	e	10 f		g
9	h	i	j	k
12	l	m	n	o

Figure 3.1

Notice that although Lisa and Rachel took the initiative, the teacher was still aware of the need to include Liam and Owain. When working in this way make sure that you draw in each child to contribute. This should ensure that everyone remains active, has an opportunity to clarify their ideas, and contributes to the group's understanding of the problem.

- A final piece of advice. Once the children have started on an activity try not to do any direct teaching. Listen carefully and push your own ideas to the back of your mind. In particular show respect for the children's ideas and try not to comment on everything that is said.

This last point does not mean that you cannot have pre-determined goals for the children or yourself, as the next example shows. The teacher is working with a group of six reception class children investigating patterns of 6. Notice that the teacher is careful to allow the children to develop their own ideas. There is ample reward in the richness of the suggestions offered by the children, and in the manner in which they share and extend each other's ideas. Nevertheless, there is still a job for the teacher to do. She listens carefully to what the children have to say and, as well as offering praise and encouragement, keeps the momentum going with a series of carefully chosen interventions. These interventions usually take the form of questions designed to keep the children thinking. They are 'open' in the sense that there is not just one 'correct' answer and this ensures that the children have the opportunity to compare and extend their own thinking further. There is also some closed questioning as the teacher demonstrates to Jonathan the difference between 'b' and 'd', and as she attempts to assess the children's understanding of conservation of number. See if you can distinguish between the types of questioning used.

[*The children are seated around a table and each child has six coloured counters.*]
Teacher: Can you make a pattern with your six counters? [*Ryan and Jonathan hesitate and watch what the others are doing.*]
Michael: Look, I've made six.

Teacher: Good boy. What pattern have you made?
Michael [*proudly*]:   It's a rectangle.
Teacher: That's very good. Has anyone else made a different pattern?
Gemma: Mine's a circle.

18 *Discussion-based teaching*

Wesley: And I've made a triangle.

Jonathan [*trying to copy this pattern*]: Mine's not – it hasn't got a pointy bit.

Michael: You haven't used six, see – you've only got five. You need one more, silly! [*Jonathan recounts and happily finishes his triangle.*]
Rhia: Look at my beautiful flower.

Gemma: It's nice.
Teacher: Good girl, Rhia.
[*Ryan hasn't said anything yet but he has made a different pattern.*]
Teacher: What have you made, Ryan?
Ryan: A 'tuh' shape.

Teacher: Good boy. Look at Ryan's 't' shape. Can we make our six counters into any more 'sound' shapes? [*There is furious activity for a few seconds.*]
Michael: Look, look – a 'l'.

Jonathan: I've made a 'd'.

Gemma: No, it's not, it's a 'b'.
Teacher: Good boy, Jonathan – if we move these two counters we can make a 'd', can't we?

Wesley [*still thinking about shapes*]: I'm going to make a square. [*The others watch him. After a few seconds he ends up with*

• • •
• • •

and looks rather puzzled.]
Gemma: No – it's a rectangle.
Michael [*Pushing Wesley's counters together*]: Now it looks like a square.

• • •
• • •

[*Wesley smiles appreciatively.*]
Teacher: Let's move all these lovely patterns into the middle where we can all look at them. They are all very nice but are they all made from six counters?
Rhia, Gemma, Michael and Wesley: Yes.
Teacher: I'll make a pattern of six now. [*She picks up six counters and, counting aloud, 'One, two, three, four, five, six', places them on the table.*]

• • • • • •

Wesley: We didn't think of that one, did we, Miss?
Teacher: Now I'll make another – [*again counting aloud*] one, two, three, four, five, six.

• • • • • •

[*The two lines of counters are placed close to one another.*]

• • • • • • • • •

Do both my patterns have the same number of counters? [*Michael, Rhia and Wesley agree without hesitation that they do. Gemma makes a quick count and both she and Ryan nod agreement. However, Jonathan looks puzzled.*]
Teacher: Are they the same number, Jonathan?
Jonathan: No – that's more [*pointing to the longer line*].
Wesley: No – she just moved those [*pointing to the longer line*] and made big gaps – they're still the same.
Gemma: They got longer but they're still six.
Teacher: Let's count and check.
Together: One, two, three, four, five, six.

Teacher: Now this line.
Together: One, two, three, four, five, six.
Teacher: Do both patterns have the same number of counters?
All: Yes.
Teacher: These patterns are so nice that it's a shame to lose them. If you are feeling very clever today, perhaps you could copy them by putting sticky paper circles onto sugar paper. Then the rest of the class can admire your work.

Summary

In this chapter we suggest that the following points be observed by those teachers who wish to begin developing a discussion-based approach.

- It is important to involve each child.
- The teacher needs to listen and observe carefully.
- It is worthwhile to move forward with the children's own ideas.
- The experienced teacher can arrive at a pre-defined goal through an apparently child-driven activity.

Notice the way in which this last point is achieved in the given example. Initially the children decided how they would arrange the counters. The teacher showed respect for their ideas, valuing all contributions and appearing interested and enthusiastic. She was prepared to exploit and extend the children's ideas before focusing attention on a pattern of her own. In this way she moved towards her implicitly defined aim of testing the children's understanding of conservation. At the end of the activity everyone was likely to feel that they had personally contributed, and to take some responsibility for the results obtained. This type of 'personalising' is much more likely to encourage children to want to 'own' the concept or skill than if it were introduced in a teacher-directed way.

Teacher activities

3.1 Carry out a discussion-based activity as outlined above. In particular,
- encourage the children to share their perceptions of the problem *before they begin* and

- show respect for the children's ideas and try to respond to them. (This does not mean you have to lose sight of where you are going!)

3.2 Consider what you have learnt about the children involved. Try to think in terms of understanding, attitudes, language, social and personal skills as described in Chapter 1.

3.3 What 'follow-up' activities present themselves? Are there any gaps in the children's understanding that require attention?

4 Evaluating Discussion Activities

Having carried out a discussion activity it is very important to reflect on what occurred. The reflective process will be enhanced if you jot down on paper some of your ideas. Written notes will help to concentrate the mind and focus attention on important issues. For example:

- Can you reconstruct and describe the general flow of the activity?
- Did all the children contribute? Were they active or passive, enthusiastic or uninterested?
- Did you learn anything new about individual children? What impressions did you form concerning their understanding and behaviour?
- Was the situation one which allowed the children to think for themselves? What follow-up activities suggest themselves? Were there any significant moments?
- Can you analyse your own part in the activity? In particular were there times when you were teaching conventionally rather than conducting discussion?

The teacher who carried out the sorting tray activity described in Chapter 2 made the following observations.

> The children were very enthusiastic and enjoyed this very basic activity. Throughout the session I found Gavin a very dominant group member and a pace-setter, while Ceri opened up new avenues to be explored in her final set of comments. I was well aware of my role in the session and attempted to provide initial information and ask challenging questions without doing the thinking for the children. I was also careful to ensure that each child was asked to contribute to the discussion, and attempted to draw out their ideas whenever possible.
>
> During the initial practical work there was not a lot of pupil–pupil interaction, but I felt that this position improved quite dramatically when the children were challenged to alter their sets. Gavin and Ceri certainly took a leading role, and some of their ideas could have been developed further or used as new starting points. However, I wanted everyone to contribute, so I was careful to make sure that each child took a turn putting forward their ideas while the others listened.
>
> I feel that the activity provided me with an opportunity to assess the group's

understanding of matching a number symbol to a set, and gave me information about the children's readiness to progress to further work.

A cassette recording can be a great help in reflection and evaluation. Try taping one of your sessions. You may be surprised by what, and how much, you have to say! However, if you or the children are unfamiliar with the use of a cassette recorder in the classroom situation, postpone its introduction until you have carried out a number of discussion activities. Children need to be relaxed and behaving naturally before any recording is of value. When you do start making recordings, allow time for the novelty to subside. Encourage children to speak clearly and describe what they are doing. Cover tables and other surfaces with material to absorb 'noise' and try to ensure that interruptions are kept to a minimum.

When you play back the cassette it is useful to complete some checklists. It will be beneficial if you draw up relevant checklists yourself. These may include the following.

Assessing yourself

- Did I do everything possible to make the children feel secure and confident?
- Did the children know what was expected of them from the start?
- Was the level of the work appropriate?
- Did I show respect by valuing the children's ideas?
- Was I able to identify the less able/able/dominant children within the group?
- Was I able to judge when to intervene with appropriate questions?

Assessing the group

- Did the children talk to each other about their work?
- Did the children listen to each other?
- Did the children share their ideas?
- Did the children compare ideas?
- Did the children enjoy the session?
- Did the children benefit from the session?

Assessing individual children within the group

- Did the child talk?
- Did the child listen to other members of the group?

24 Discussion-based teaching

- Did the child share ideas?
- Did the child attempt to promote and secure collaboration?
- Did the child attempt to direct the actions of other members?
- Was the child able to handle differences of opinion within the group?
- Was the child willing to defend his point of view?
- Was the child prepared to hold onto those views which were not popular with other members?
- Was the child able to predict what might happen when ... ?
- Did the child have a sense of humour or an individuality which found expression in the activity?

As well as using the cassettes for evaluation purposes, you might consider playing back the recordings to the children. In our experience this has proved most worthwhile, and has provided the children with further opportunities to develop their discussion skills.

A discussion activity might also be evaluated by considering the opportunities it provides to assess and enhance the understanding, language, and personal skills of the children involved. With this in mind we have devised the evaluation sheet shown in 6.4 (p. 43). After carrying out a discussion activity and engaging in a period of reflection the teacher completes the speech bubbles by writing in relevant statements, questions, or comments made by the children. We have used this idea to evaluate both the group activity and the performance of individual children. In the case of the group only one sheet is required and *any* child's contribution may be used. When considering individual children then one sheet per child is used. Figure 4.1 shows a completed evaluation sheet for a 7-year-old, Zoe, who had been involved in a dice-rolling investigation with a group of top infants. The fact that the teacher was able to complete all the bubbles indicates that Zoe was an active participant, while the quality of her contributions can be judged from the teacher's recording. You might like to use this sheet or a similar one to help you evaluate some of your discussion activities.

As your skills in discussion-based teaching develop, you will find that you no longer need, or wish, to tape-record sessions. Nevertheless, it is useful to keep brief notes about your discussion activities. Such notes can be written up in the form of a summary sheet (see 6.5, p. 44), and a collection of such sheets will provide a useful resource for future reference by both you and your colleagues. An example of a possible summary sheet is shown in Figure 4.2. You may want to modify this sheet into a form which is suitable for your purposes.

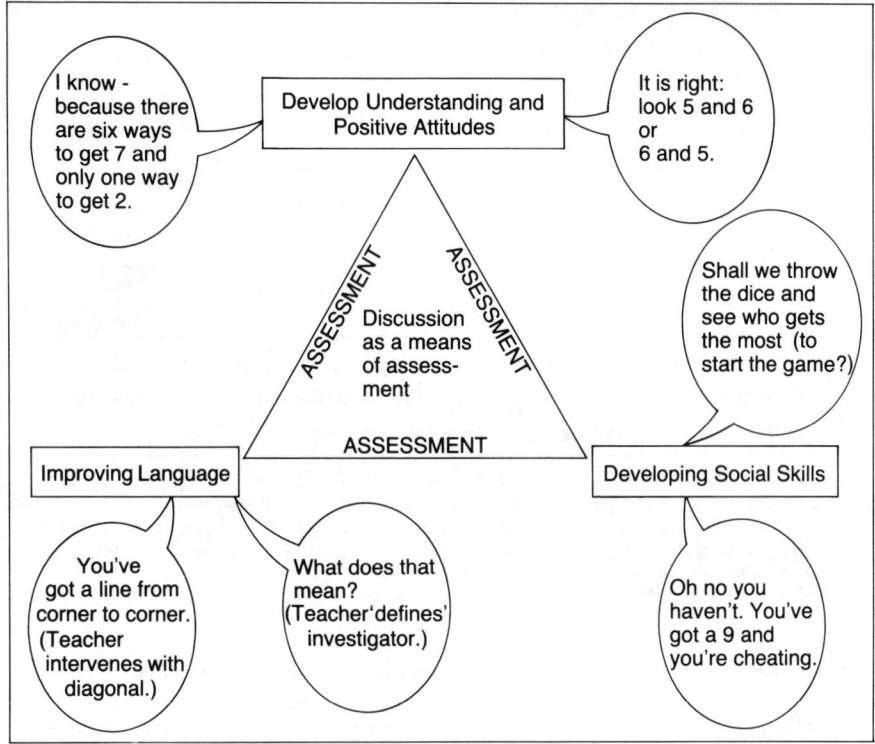

Figure 4.1

Summary

- It is important to reflect upon classroom experience.
- A variety of practical suggestions have been offered to help the teacher enhance this aspect of the learning process.
- The use of a cassette recorder, checklists, evaluation and summary sheets have been considered.

Teacher activities

4.1 Reflect on the discussion-based activity you carried out after reading Chapter 3. Write some notes which address the issues raised on page 22.

4.2 Try drawing up checklists to help you during discussion work. Carry out further discussion activities and complete the checklists. (If possible make cassette recordings to help you.)

26 *Discussion-based teaching*

CLASS	NUMBER IN GROUP	TYPE OF GROUP	TEACHER DIRECTED/ CHILD CENTRED	AREA OF MATHEMATICS
Middle Infants	5	same ability	Free Choice	Peak Comparative language

AIM
① To get the children to talk about mathematics
② To improve the quality of the mathematics in the group.
③ To get the children to co-operate – work together

METHOD The children were seated in a group but working individually from peak work cards – very little mathematical thinking taking place. The teacher joined the group and directed the children to the one card – asked the question "Let's have a look at Charlene's card – what can you tell me about your card Charlene?"

EXAMPLE OF DIALOGUE

Christopher – There's one, two, three, four elephants, one big one and one, two, three little ones.

Jacqueline – "Oh Christopher you don't have to count them like that you can see there are four just by looking"

Peter – "Well look at mine – I've got seven and you've got to count them haven't you. There's lots of trees. Look Big ones, Middle size and small.

The children carried on with discussion and full account is available.

COMMENTS

There was an evident change in the quality of pupil/pupil interaction once the teacher joined the group.
From the short example of dialogue – you can see that the children are at different stages as far as their concept of number is concerned.
Later on in the session the teacher pursues the question of the child's use of comparative language and is able to make an assessment of their understanding.

VOCABULARY

long/short, number words, big/middle size/small bigger than, longer than, shorter than etc.

Figure 4.2

4.3 Evaluate some of your discussion-based activities using a sheet similar to the one shown in 6.4. Modify the sheet to suit your own purposes.

4.4 Complete some summary sheets which could be kept as a record of your discussion activities.

5 Planning and Organising Discussion

In Chapter 3 it was suggested that you should begin your discussion work with a single group of children. As your skill in handling discussion develops, you will want to extend the activity to include all of the children in your class. This can best be achieved by dividing your children into a number of distinct groups and planning your week so that each group is exposed to some practical work which involves discussion with the teacher. In order to gain the most from these sessions you will need to 'timetable' yourself to work with each group in turn.

Timetabling

A typical organisational pattern is illustrated in Figure 5.1. The teacher has divided her class into four ability groups (Red, Yellow, Blue and Green) and has timetabled herself to work with each group on a rota basis. The groupings are flexible and children are moved between them when necessary.

During any one of the morning sessions the teacher plans to work with two groups; typically one of them will be doing and talking about some mathematics, while the other will be engaged in some aspect of language or science work. The teacher divides the majority of her time between these two groups (discussing, observing, listening, encouraging, and assessing) and spends only a small proportion of her time monitoring the remaining groups. These remaining groups will also be involved in language, science and mathematical work, but the activities will be less dependent on the teacher's immediate involvement. Suitable activities, which are often presented as a series of tasks, might involve workbooks or workcards, practising handwriting skills, constructional play, mathematical games and puzzles, practical measuring, pattern work, shopping and other role-play situations. Work begun in teacher-contact sessions may spill over into these 'free-choice' periods which can also

Planning and organising 29

	Monday	Tuesday	Wednesday	Thursday	Friday
9:00–9:15	Greetings and registration				
9:15–10:10	Red (T) / Yellow — Blue / (T) Green	Yellow (T) / Red — Green / (T) Blue	Green (T) / Blue — Yellow / (T) Red	Blue (T) / Green — Red / (T) Yellow	Red / Yellow — Blue / Green
10:10–10:20	Class activity/review of previous session				
10:20–10:30	Break time				
10:30–10:50	School assembly				
10:50–11:45	Yellow (T) / Red — Green / (T) Blue	Red (T) / Yellow — Blue / (T) Green	Blue (T) / Green — Red / (T) Yellow	Green (T) / Blue — Yellow / (T) Red	Yellow / Red — Green / Blue
11:45–11:55	Class activity/review of previous session				

Notes:
1. The teacher is timetabled to work with those groups indicated by T.
2. Groups are involved mainly with language, science and mathematical activity – the timetable needs to be balanced according to content.
3. The afternoon pattern is similar but with more emphasis on creative, recreational, environmental and thematic work.

Figure 5.1

be used to record earlier experiences or provide additional opportunities for exploration and consolidation.

The afternoon sessions are similar in nature but there is more emphasis on creative work, environmental work, and theme development. Again, work begun during discussion activities in the morning may well continue as cross-curricular links are developed and exploited.

Within the teacher-contact periods there is also a need for flexibility. Groups may be further divided into fours, threes, or pairs; individual needs also have to be catered for. Friday mornings are not timetabled in quite the same way as the rest of the week, and allow for the tying-up of loose ends, consolidation, class discussion, and reflection.

Classroom organisation

To be successful, the classroom itself must support the group method of working. Management of space (the placement of furniture and working areas) and resources are important issues. In particular the mathematics area should contain all the apparatus and materials the children are likely to require, while the background displays should include examples of the children's work, appropriate charts, and reference materials. Children should be encouraged to take responsibility for getting out (and putting away!) the materials they require. These should be readily available on clearly labelled shelves or in easily accessed cupboards, and should be valued both by the teacher and pupils. Since mathematical apparatus is often at a premium within schools, it may be a good idea to discuss your requirements with other members of staff and draw up a timetable for its use. In this way you could concentrate on one particular aspect of the curriculum (say, Shape) over a period of time, while colleagues work on other topics using apparatus you do not need. Efficient management of resources in this way is beneficial to all and is a matter that curriculum coordinators might like to address.

Stages of the activity

The mathematical activity itself must also support this method of working. It may include various combinations of:

Planning and organising 31

- discussion between children and teacher
- some thinking and discussion time without the teacher
- some time for activity and the trying out of ideas (with or without the teacher)
- some recording activity involving individuals, pairs or the whole group (usually without the teacher)

These stages are not intended to be sequential and a typical session may involve an interplay in which the children revisit one or more of the stages on a number of occasions. The teacher works closely with the group for only part of the timetabled session and is free to attend to the needs of the second group or the rest of the children during the remaining period.

As an illustration of this type of interaction consider again the addition activity described in Chapter 3 (pp. 16–17). The initial discussion and the subsequent development of ideas led to a period of unsupervised pupil activity in which a worksheet was completed. During this time the teacher was able to work with a second group before returning to extend the ideas of the children by challenging

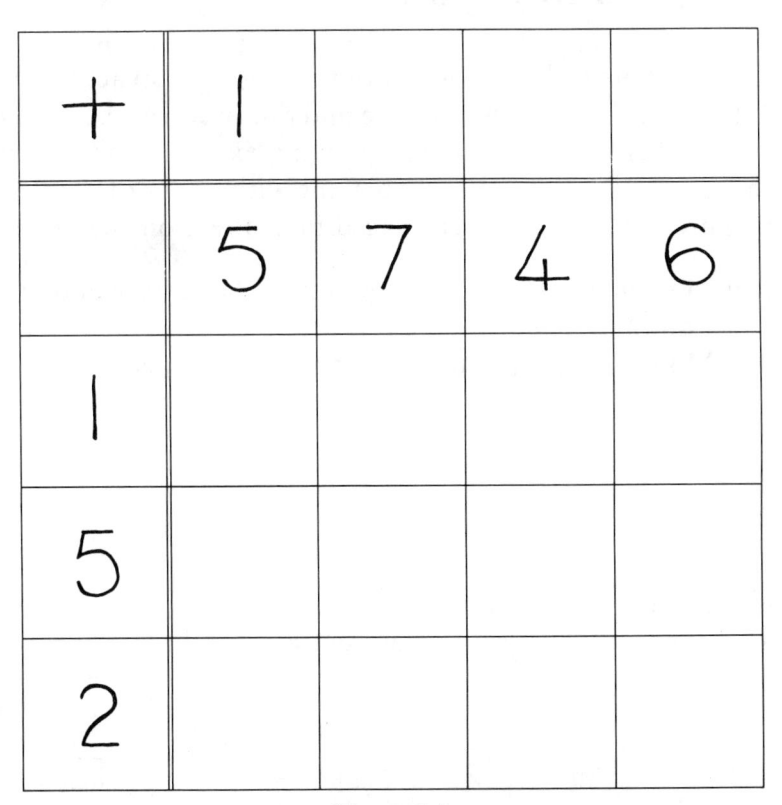

+	1			
	5	7	4	6
1				
5				
2				

Figure 5.2

32 Discussion-based teaching

them to predict what would happen if the 8 on the worksheet (see Figure 3.1) was changed to a 9. The discussion that followed eventually led to the teacher presenting the children with a second worksheet (see Figure 5.2) which again allowed her to move on to another group.

There are many variations possible for this follow-up worksheet. You might use different numbers or change the operation (subtraction instead of addition – 'which do we take away?'). Again you could vary the position of the given numbers and answers. All of this should lead to profitable discussion and provide additional time for the teacher to work with other groups. Finally, the children might construct worksheets for each other which they could compare and check themselves. This proved very popular with one class and resulted in many children electing to continue with the work into their free-choice sessions, thus helping further with classroom organisation.

Turning it into a game

Alternatively there is the possibility of turning a group activity into a game which becomes self-supporting and thus releases the teacher to work with other children. In the following example four reception class children and their teacher are playing with a pack of home-made pattern cards which have been placed face down on the table.

Teacher: I want you to take a card, look at the pattern and find the number label to match it.
Emma: Miss, I've got a 4 pattern and here's a 4 card.

Rachel: I've got a 3 pattern.
Teacher: Let's all look at Rachel's pattern carefully.

Simon: It's not a 3 pattern, it's a 4 pattern. There's 1 in the corner, she forgot that 1.

Gavin: Miss, I've got a 5 pattern and I need a 5 card.

Emma: No, you haven't. You haven't got 1 in the middle. [*Emma's idea of 5 is probably* .]

Gavin: It don't matter, I got 3 in that line and 2 in that line, that's one, two, three, four, five altogether.

Emma: Miss, this is 5 pattern because there's 1 in the middle [*produces a card similar to the one shown above*].

Teacher: Yes, that's right, Emma, but can we all see that Gavin's is a 5 pattern also?

Rachel: This is a 5 pattern. Look, Miss, 3 down this line and 1 in this corner and 1 in this corner. That's 5.

Gavin: Yes, but there's a set of 2 there, and another set of 2 as well, and that's 4 altogether. 2 and 2 makes 4. [*Gavin indicates that he is referring to the top and bottom rows on the card which each includes two objects. The teacher decides to encourage this line of development and shows them another 5 pattern.*]

Teacher: Well, what can you all tell me about this pattern?
Gavin: Miss, it's a 1 and a 2 and a 2.
Rachel: Miss, it's a 5 pattern. 3 on the bottom and 2 on top of them.
Emma: Miss, there's one missing.
Teacher: Tell us what you mean, Emma.
Emma: There's one missing from here. If you had 1 more you'd have a 6 pattern.

There is much of interest here, and the situation is one which can be exploited further by taking advantage of the children's different perceptions. This could be achieved by building a game around the activity. Games can be a very effective way of generating doing, talking and recording, and they will usually have the advantage of releasing the teacher for much of the time. It is also extremely helpful to incorporate a *systematic-talk element* into a game situation thus increasing the opportunities for discussion. This can be done very simply by making each player justify her or his move and requiring the other players to agree or to challenge. Games like this engage the children in working with ideas over an extended period rather than rushing from one workcard to the next. Such fleeting experiences, although helpful at the time, may be shallowly founded and quickly forgotten. Try to devise games which are based around learning materials such as rods, squared paper, Unifix cubes and the like. Memory games are common, but are only useful for memorising and cannot develop understanding.

To include these features in the above activity we might proceed as follows.

- Prepare a set of pattern cards. You may wish to investigate one particular number (Figure 5.3).
- Seat the children comfortably in a circle around a table or on the floor.
- Make sure that all the apparatus needed is readily to hand. In this activity, as well as the pattern cards, it might be useful to provide counters or Unifix blocks as aids to counting and/or the recognition of patterns.
- Explain clearly what is required. Remember that it is useful to get the children to demonstrate their understanding of your explanation by asking each of them to show you what they have to do before starting the game proper. This will allow for some *negotiation of meaning*, as the children may initially have quite different perceptions of what is required by the teacher's instructions.
- Allow the children to decide who is to start. Suppose Emma is chosen; she turns up the first card.
- To score a point Emma must now make an appropriate statement about the card, which must be accepted by the other players. If her statement is incorrect and is challenged successfully by another player who can also provide a correct statement, then the point is scored by the challenger.

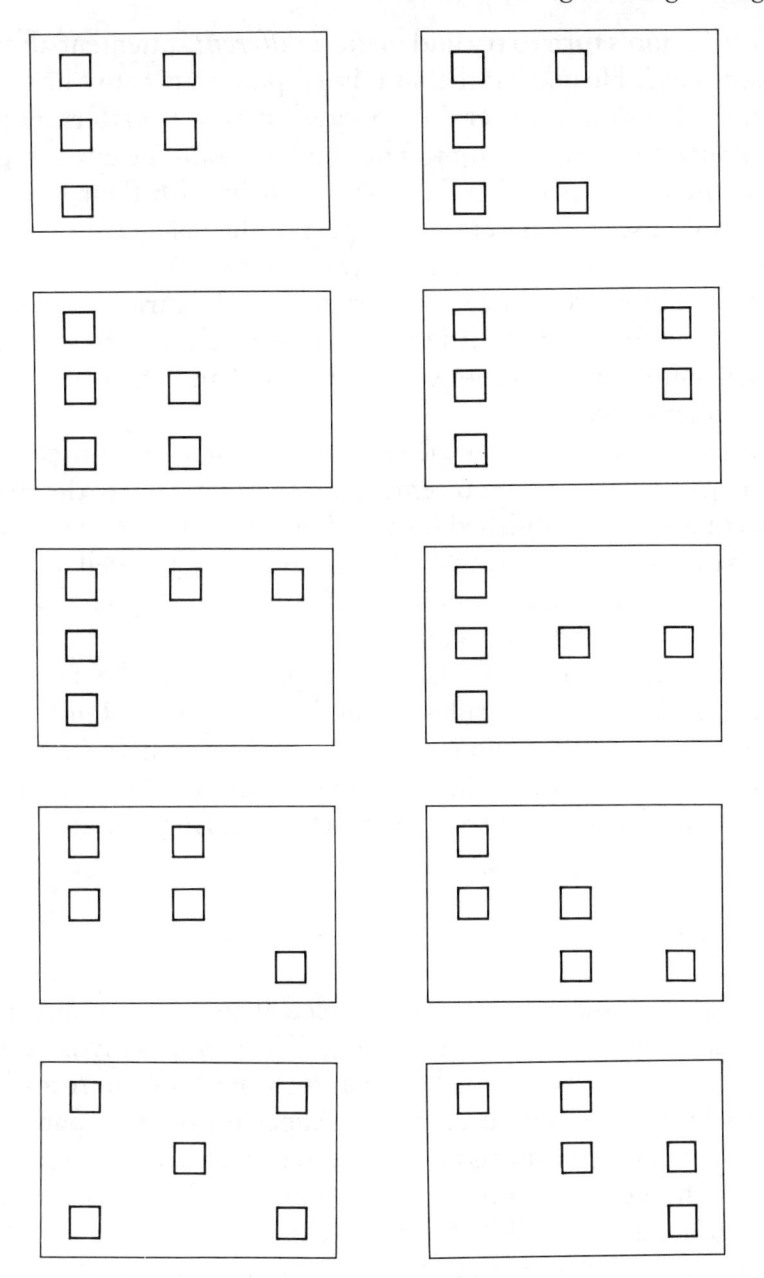

Figure 5.3 These are some possible pattern cards to make for investigating 5. There is an interesting investigation here regarding the number of different cards that can be made. How many possibilities can you find? Some patterns can be obtained by rotating others – can you spot the duplicates here?

- An appropriate statement might simply be that it is a 5 pattern. However, if the child is also required to justify the statement then the situation is greatly enhanced. For example, Emma might say that it is a 5 pattern 'because I can see a 3 and a 2 pattern'. It is now Simon's turn to try and make a *different* statement about the same card. He may state that it is a 5 pattern because he sees 'a 2 and a 1 and a 2 pattern' or because it is 'a 6 pattern with a 1 missing' to score his point. The children could be encouraged to use the counters or Unifix blocks to help with their reasoning; careful observation here on the part of the teacher should reveal much about the children's understanding.

- The children are allowed to continue to take turns making statements about the *first* card until no new results can be found. It is then Simon's turn to choose a further card and attempt to make a statement about it.
- Initially the children may need help to familiarise themselves with the game and its requirements. However, once the routine becomes well established it should be possible to leave the group and direct your attention elsewhere. A number of well-structured activities like this will help considerably with your classroom organisation and management.
- Be flexible in terms of what you expect. Allow the situation to evolve and change the rules to suit the needs of the children. (You may well find that the children take the initiative here!) With older children you might well expect them to *state*, *justify*, and *write* an appropriate statement before scoring a point.

Recording

Finally, class management can be aided if groups are directed to 'record' the work they have been doing. The children involved in the cube-rolling activity described in Chapter 1 were able to record their patterns by sticking coloured paper shapes onto sugar paper. The teacher had planned for this and all the materials needed were readily to hand. This ensured a further opportunity for that teacher to move on to another group of children. Careful planning, the availability of materials and the encouragement of pupil responsibility are all important considerations in the development of an effective learning environment.

Summary

- The organisational implications of introducing more 'talk' into the classroom have been considered.

- Practical suggestions have been offered which allow time for teacher–pupil as well as pupil–pupil discussion.
- The idea of a self-supporting activity which incorporates a systematic-talk element has been introduced.

Teacher activities

5.1 Consider how you might organise your working day or week to allow for discussion-based teaching. Draw up a timetable to indicate which groups you would be working with at various times. How would you balance your content to ensure adequate coverage of all subject areas?

5.2 Plan a mathematical activity which will allow you to spend some time working with a group (discussing, observing, listening, encouraging and assessing) and which also provides some non-contact time in which you might join a second group or monitor the remainder of your class.

5.3 Select an activity (perhaps 'Pattern Cards' described above) and introduce it to a group of children. Attempt to develop it into a self-supporting activity with a systematic-talk element. Be sure to encourage the children to check all statements and moves.

6 Sharing Ideas – Some Inset Activities

Throughout the earlier chapters we have stressed the importance of encouraging children to share and compare their ideas in order to develop understanding and personal skills. The same philosophy is equally important in the case of teacher and curriculum development. Although the teacher activities suggested throughout this book can be used on an individual basis, their value will be enhanced if they are carried out by a group or pair of teachers who are prepared to share their experiences. To help with the planning and implementation of such a staff development programme, we offer the following suggestions which are supported by the photocopiable resource material provided on pages 40–44.

- Teacher group meets to consider reasons why discussion in mathematics should be considered important. Are the reasons presented in Chapter 1 acceptable? What other benefits might there be? Teacher activities 1.1 and 1.2 can be used as a focus for discussion, while it is also recommended that the group should engage in some mathematics at their own level. An investigation of the number bonds of 5 (see page 7) or a problem-solving activity such as finding the number of squares on a chess-board might be appropriate. In either case the emphasis should be on sharing ideas rather than on searching for an 'answer'.
- Group members work together to draw up a list of ways in which a teacher might use language in the classroom (see 2.1). What is meant by 'discussion'? Members read and discuss the case studies presented in 6.1 (see pages 40 and 41). How did the two teachers differ in their approaches? What is meant by 'open' and 'closed' questions (see 2.2)? Can the group identify examples of these types of questions in the case studies? Members work together to draw up a list of questions which they might ask in the classroom and classify them as open or closed.
- Group members carry out a teaching activity as described in Chapter 3. After a period of individual reflection members report back to the group on their own experiences. Section 6.2 can be

photocopied to help individuals with the planning of their activity, while 6.3 is provided as a focus for the reporting-back stage.
- Individuals carry out further discussion activities and make cassette recordings of teacher–pupil and pupil–pupil interaction. These recordings can then be used for further reflection and group discussion.
- Group members work together to draw up checklists and complete evaluation and summary sheets as described in Chapter 4. Copies of blank worksheets are included in 6.4 and 6.5.
- Group considers the organisational and resource implications of introducing more discussion work into their teaching. How could 'Take Thirty' (see 6.1b) be developed into a self-supporting activity?

Resource material for Inset activities

This material is photocopiable and copies should be made available to each member of the Inset group.

6.1 Two case studies

Read, compare and discuss the following snippets of classroom talk.

a 'Forty-two Take away Twenty-five'

A class of lower juniors was working individually from teacher-prepared worksheets. Rhys was having problems.

Teacher: Now, from 42 it says take away 25. Let's start with the 5. 5 from 2; can you do that?
Rhys: No.
Teacher: Why not? Why can't you do it?
Rhys: Two ones.
Teacher: You've only got two ones, haven't you? You haven't got enough. Remember what we did last time when we didn't have enough?
Rhys: ... Uhm ...
Teacher: What did we have to do?
Rhys: You take the ... uhm ... that ...
Teacher: You had to borrow. What did we have to borrow?
Rhys: 3 ...
Teacher: 3? Did you have to borrow 3? 5 from 2? You've got four tens and two ones. What do you have to borrow?
Rhys: 4? ... no, 1 ...

b 'Take Thirty'

This game is played with five ten rods (Cuisenaire or Dienes), twenty-five unit cubes, and an ordinary die. The two players take turns throwing the die and collecting the number of cubes corresponding to that shown on the die. The winner is the first child to obtain thirty or more cubes.

Barrie: Miss, Gavin needs five and there's only three ones left.
Teacher: What do you think he could do about that? How many cubes have you got, Gavin?
Gavin: Miss, twelve.

Barrie: I've got an idea. He could change ten ones for a ten rod and then we'll have the ones back again.
Teacher: Why not! Try it, Gavin.
Gavin: Um ... that's a good idea. I've got twelve ... that's one ten and two units, so I've got enough.
Barrie: I've thrown a six. I could take them but I could change them as well because I've got more than ten.

As the game continued the children became very enthusiastic about the possibilities that an exchange might present. Instead of regrouping their unit cubes into tens for the exchange they were keen to take a ten rod and 'pay back' from their own pile of unit cubes.

Gavin: Miss, I've got twenty-seven now. I only need three more to make thirty. Barrie, how many more do you need?
Barrie: I need six because I've got twenty-four. It's my turn. I've got a five so now I need one more to win.
Gavin: Hooray, I've got three so I've won.
Barrie: Miss, he beat me by one.

6.2 Getting started

- Before the next meeting arrange to do some mathematics with a group of children from your class.
- Sit with the children and encourage them to talk about the work they are doing.
- Listen carefully to what they have to say and try to ensure that each child contributes.
- Ask the children to explain their ideas, showing respect for their opinions.
- Try not to comment on everything that the children say. Instead draw in other members of the group to share their views.
- If you do need to intervene to keep things going then try to ask a 'What if ... ?' or a 'Can you show me?' type of question.
- Afterwards, *reflect* and *record*. Make notes (which should be available at the next meeting) reconstructing the general 'flow' of the session, and comment on any significant matters. For example:
  - Did all the children contribute? Were they active or passive, enthusiastic or uninterested?
  - What impressions did you form concerning understanding and behaviour? Were the children cooperative, withdrawn, dominating?

- Did the situation enable the children to develop their own mathematical thinking? What follow-up activities presented themselves?
- Can you analyse your own part in the activity? In particular were there times when you were teaching conventionally rather than conducting discussion?

6.3 Reporting back – Some starting points for discussion

1. Describe briefly the activity you planned and the way in which it was organised. How did the session develop?
2. How easy or difficult was it to reconstruct the session afterwards? Were you able to recall the significant moments and the main contributions made by each of the children?
3. Did the situation encourage the children to think? Were they prepared to talk and listen to each other?
4. What impressions did you form concerning behaviour, understanding, and group interaction? Were there any surprises?
5. Were the suggestions made in 6.2 useful? To what extent do you think you followed them? (Be honest!)
6. Can you analyse your own part in the activity? Were there times when you were teaching conventionally rather than conducting discussion?
7. Do you think the experience was a worthwhile and enjoyable one for you and/or the children? What were the advantages and disadvantages?
8. Is this style of teaching one that you have used regularly in the past, or is it quite new to you? What is your overall impression of the approach?

6.4 An evaluation sheet

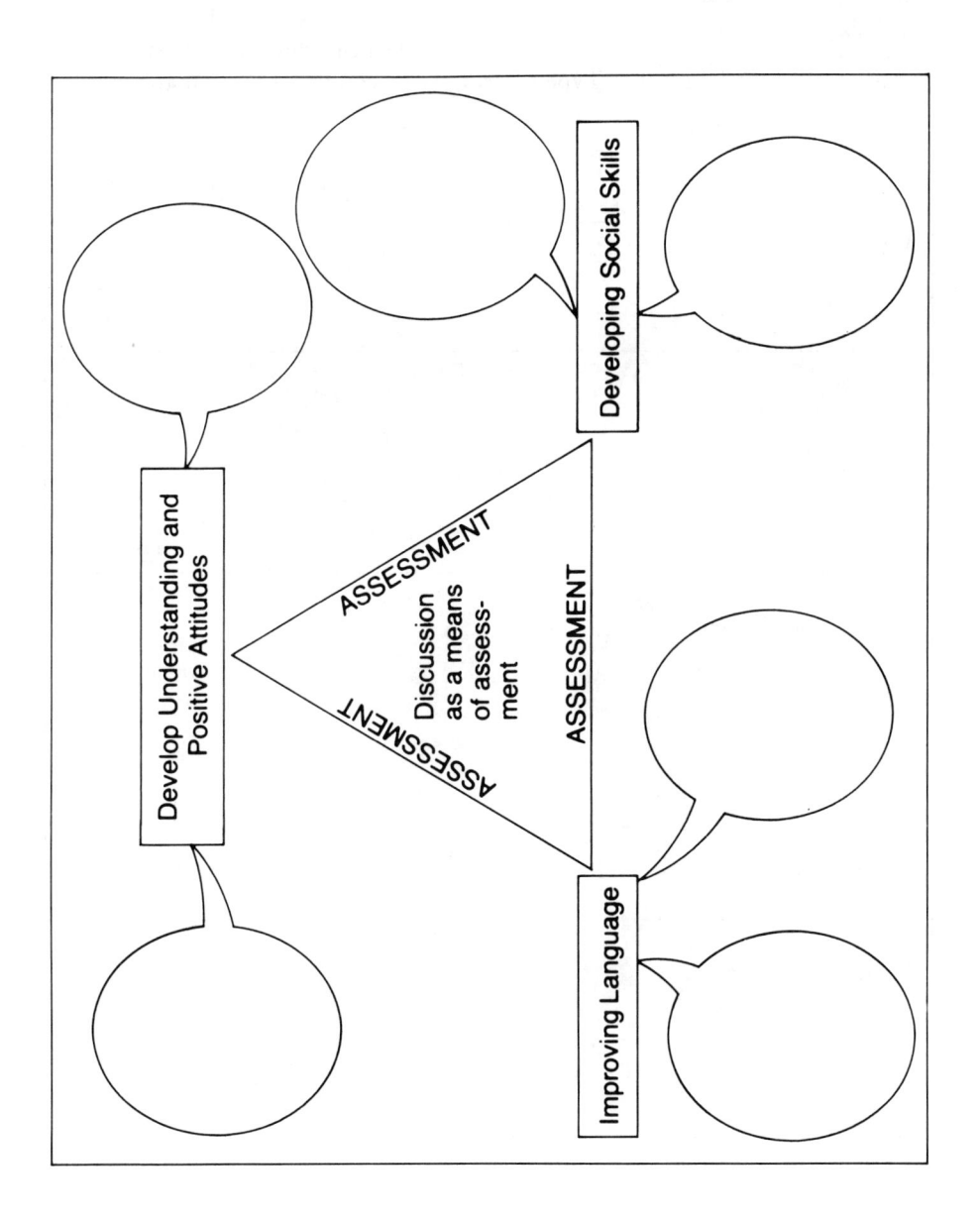

6.5 Summary sheet

Class	Number in group	Type of group	Teacher-directed or child-centred	Area of mathematics

Aim

Method

Example of dialogue

Comments

Vocabulary

Part Two

A RESOURCE PACK FOR DEVELOPING A DISCUSSION-BASED APPROACH

7 Handling Mathematical Discussion – A Summary of Key Ideas

The way in which a teacher handles discussion is crucial to the development of any mathematical activity. In this chapter we have collected together some of the main issues that teachers need to be aware of when using a discussion-based approach. In order that the information provided is of manageable proportions we have kept the number of points made as small as possible. Each section has been labelled for later reference (see Chapter 8) and all points need to be borne in mind when planning and handling discussion work. To familiarise yourself with the ideas presented it would be useful to conduct a series of group sessions concentrating on just one or two points per session.

7.1 Use open-ended activities and ask challenging questions

A basic principle to bear in mind is the need to encourage children to develop their own ideas. In discussion work there needs to be a shift away from the teacher doing the thinking and an emphasis on getting the children involved. Consequently, activities which can be developed (by the children!) in a variety of ways are best. When introducing such activities try and ask challenging questions, and attempt to appear genuinely interested and enthusiastic. Remember, children will need *time* if they are going to think, so do not expect immediate replies or solutions. Be prepared for periods of silence and uncertainty, and try to help in such instances by encouraging the children to share their ideas rather than by giving them answers.

7.2 Provide a focal point for discussion

When introducing an activity it is important to ensure that everyone is involved and shares an understanding of the problem (see Chapter 3). Provide apparatus and materials whenever possible as it is much easier to get children to talk about something that they have to do. When joining a group who are already at work it can be useful to focus attention on one child's ideas before asking group members for comments and further suggestions.

> 'Let's all look at
> Gavin's card.
> Can you tell us what
> you have done, Gavin?'

> 'Everyone listen to
> Charlene. Tell us
> what you have been
> doing, Charlene.'

7.3 Allow children time to develop their own ideas

Show respect for the children's ideas and allow them to personalise their experiences. If you openly evaluate and comment on everything the children say and do, then any discussion will quickly degenerate into a conventional question-and-answer session with the children attempting to provide answers which are judged as being 'correct' by the teacher. Avoid taking over the session; encourage the children themselves to evaluate and comment on each other's ideas.

> 'What do you think
> of Gemma's idea? ...
> Jonathan? ...
> Michael? ...'

> 'Does everyone agree
> with that? What do
> you think, Jonathan? ...
> Michael? ...'

Holding back, particularly when you judge that an idea is useful, or that the children have not really grasped what is required, can be very difficult. However, it can also be very rewarding if the children are able to negotiate their own understanding out of the experience provided. You can often help this process by emphasising or extending the children's observations.

> 'Terry, that was
> interesting. Can
> you say it again,
> only more slowly
> please?'

> 'Mary is saying ...
> Does that
> mean ... ?'

If this is not successful then you can always take over and clarify later; so if in doubt, hold back!

7.4 Encourage children to share and compare ideas

This, of course, is the essence of discussion and is at the heart of the learning process. The suggestions made above are designed to aid this process, while suitable other interventions by the teacher might be along the following lines.

'Does everyone agree? ... Has anyone got another way of doing it? ... What about you, David? ... Katie? ...'

'O.K., that's John's view. Now what ideas have you got? ... Jonathan? ... Michael? ...'

When drawing in children to share ideas, try and make sure that you vary the order in which you identify them. Thus if Amanda, Barry, Claire and David have contributed (in that order) in one round of sharing, try to contrive that Barry, Claire, David and Amanda's contributions form the second (or a later) round. In this way each individual has the opportunity to express his/her views first, and all of the children are kept active.

An extension of the above idea is to develop a game around an activity and incorporate a systematic-talk element (see Chapter 5). In such an extension each child takes a turn, makes a move, and justifies the move by articulating (and possibly recording) a suitable statement. The move and statement are open to challenge and debate by the other group members, thus keeping everyone involved. Activities which have been adapted in this way can become self-supporting and release the teacher to spend time working with other groups of children, thus aiding classroom organisation.

7.5 Keep the children involved

Once the children are thinking (and talking) keep them active. Try to ask questions which enable the children to identify important features, recognise relevant properties, or use appropriate language. If you get asked a direct question, try to deflect it or redirect it at other children. Phrases such as:

'That's an interesting question, Kelly. What do *you* think?'   or   'Everyone listen. Say that again, Kelly, so we can all think about it.'

are useful in this respect.

50 Resource pack

You will need to keep track of those children who have contributed and those who are reluctant to speak. This is no different to conventional question and answer and you should react accordingly. For example, you may want to draw in a quiet child or give someone else a chance:

'We haven't heard from you yet, Simon.'   or   'Right, Jeremy, you've had a lot to say. It's Mary's turn now.'

To ensure that all the children are kept thinking, it is useful to qualify any probing questions you may ask with a phrase such as:

'Now I want you all to think about that. Don't say anything yet. I'll ask you all again in a few moments.'

After a suitable period of thinking time ask each of the children for their ideas and comments. Direct your attention towards each child in turn making sure that you vary your starting point each time you use the strategy. This should keep all the children 'on their toes' and provide each child with the opportunity of presenting ideas first.

7.6 Ask questions to assess understanding

As well as keeping the children thinking, it is important for you, as a teacher, to find out as much as possible about each child's understanding. Prompts such as

'Tell us what you are doing, Jane.'   or   'Tell us why you did that, Brian.'

or   'Can you explain why you did/said that?'

help children to clarify and extend their own ideas, and provide valuable information for assessment purposes. More searching questions, such as:

Summary of key ideas 51

| 'Why do you think that happened?' | or | 'What if we ... ?' |

or   'Why can't we ... ?'

should also be used to gain insight into the children's understanding, and to test whether the children are able to transfer their learning to related situations.

7.7 Ask helpful questions to aid progress

Questions can also be used in a helpful way to link ideas together, to aid progress or to allow children to clarify their own thinking. A group of 6-year-olds were considering the use of the words 'long' and 'short'.

Peter: I can see 'Spotty Man'. He is long going up, but he's not as long as the classroom – that's longer, and it's very big, too.
Charlene: Yes, but what about the cupboard?
Christopher: It's nearly as long as the classroom.
Jaqueline: The pencils are long as well.
Teacher: You said the cupboard is long, the classroom is long, and the pencils are long as well. Are you saying that they are *all* long?
Charlene: No, the pencil is short by the side of the cupboard. Look!

With this Charlene held her pencil alongside the cupboard thus affording the children an opportunity to appreciate more fully the relative nature of this particular concept. Notice that it was the teacher's intervention that prompted this action, and that her question, although helpful, was carefully worded to avoid doing the thinking for the children.

7.8 Use conventional teaching when required

Although in the above example the teacher's intervention produced the desired results, this will not always be so. There may well be situations in which the teacher needs to step in and take over with some conventional teaching. Vocabulary and language patterns may have to be introduced in this way, although it is often possible for the teacher to 'inject' such usage through the discussion itself. Again, new skills and concepts may need some formal input, although anything totally outside the children's experience is almost certainly inappropriate as teaching material.

8 Discussion Activities

This chapter includes a variety of discussion activities that have worked well for us. They are presented in five separate sections using headings adopted within the National Curriculum – Number, Algebra, Measures, Shape and Space, and Handling Data – and linked with specific attainment targets described there. However, it is important to appreciate that work carried out within one content area, or material which is directed at one target, will undoubtedly influence and broaden children's experience of mathematics as a whole. Consequently, it is too simplistic to think in terms of separate activities for distinct purposes; each experience given will interact one with another to allow children to negotiate a fuller understanding of the whole. Each section includes case study material, related activities and suggestions for modified and extended work.

The case studies are intended to serve as illustrative examples of discussion work in the classroom situation. In some instances the teacher's role is highlighted by linking relevant interventions and strategies with the key ideas summarised in Chapter 7. Where this occurs the reader will be invited to refer to a particular section by an entry such as '(7.3)' – that is, 'see Section 7.3 of Chapter 7.' Where no such entry is made the reader may find it instructive to consider which of the key ideas the teacher had in mind when making an intervention or asking a question – this can prove to be a useful Inset activity.

Some of the case studies also include references to the levels of attainment specified within the National Curriculum. These references are intended as a general indication of the appropriateness of a particular activity and it is important to realise that children can attain at more than one level when engaged in discussion-based work. Indeed, most of the activities suggested in this book should work well at a variety of levels, as the emphasis is on encouraging children to develop and share their own ideas. When evaluating discussion it is recommended that the assessment opportunities discussed in Chapter 1 are borne in mind, and that evaluation and summary sheets similar to those introduced in Chapter 6 are produced. It is our experience that this can be a great help in building up individual profiles of children.

The activities and extensions, along with the case studies, are provided as a resource which readers can call upon when using a discussion style in their own classrooms. No attempt has been made to provide an exhaustive coverage of the primary mathematics syllabus. The examples given are merely possible starting points for developing a discussion-based approach and as such should be used to supplement work done within a school's mathematics scheme and not to replace it.

Again no specific activities for Attainment Targets 1 and 9 (Using and applying mathematics) have been given. These targets require that:

> Pupils should use – number, algebra and measures
> – shape and space and handle data in practical tasks, in real-life problems, and to investigate within mathematics itself.

Using a discussion-based approach with a range of activities similar to the ones described in this book will, we believe, enable children to realise these aims.

Discussion activities 55

Number

Attainment Target 2 – Pupils should read and understand number and number notation

Grab a Group	page 55
What's the Number?	57
Number Dump	58

Attainment Target 3 – Pupils should understand number operations (addition, subtraction, multiplication and division) and make use of appropriate methods of calculation

Using the Equaliser Balance	page 60
Trio Tricks	62
Arithmogons	63
Star Number 1	67
Star Number 2	68
3, 5, 7	69

Attainment Target 4 – Pupils should estimate and approximate number

Boxes	page 70
Across the River	71

Grab a Group

- You will need a collection of buttons, counters, blocks, or other sorting materials.
- Each child 'grabs' a handful of objects and sorts them.

Case study

In this Level 1 activity five reception class children were asked to 'grab a group' from a box containing a large quantity of buttons of various colours, sizes, and styles. Initially there was plenty of action as the children sorted their counters onto plain sheets of paper. Some children counted, some talked about colour, all seemed to sort into twos. Chris was no exception, but he had three black buttons left over.

Teacher: Tell us about yours, Chris. (7.2)
Chris: I had 2 and 2 and 2 – all of them in twos and the blacks three.
Andrew: He's put the green to the green, red to red, the blue to the blue, yellow to the yellow, and black to the black.
Mazziar: He doesn't need this one. [*Picks up a square black button and puts it back into the box. Chris says nothing.*]
Teacher: Put all the buttons back in and try and do it a different way. (7.1)
[*The children grab groups of buttons and sort them onto their papers. There is plenty of talk as they are doing it.*]
Andrew: Miss, I've finished mine. I put three greens in there and I put one blue there, two reds there – I don't know what colour that is.
Teacher: It's the same as the table – fawn.
Andrew: One fawn and one orange.
Teacher: How many did you use altogether?
Andrew: 1, 2, 3, 4, 5, 6, 7, 8.
Jayne: I've got all different colours in the groups.
Teacher: Jayne has got different colours inside her groups. Look at the way Jayne has grouped hers. How many in this group?
All: 1, 2, 3, 4, 5.
Teacher: So how has she sorted hers?
Chris: Into numbers. 1 in there, 2 in there, 3 in there, 4 in there, and 5 in there! [*All the children find this amusing and laugh.*]
Andrew: I'm doing numbers now. 1 in there, 2 in there, 3 in there. 1, 2, 3, 4 in there, 1, 2, 3, 4, 5 in there.

Comments

Once Jayne had grouped her sets of buttons into 'numbers' the other children, led by Andrew, wanted to do the same. They enjoyed repeating this activity over a period of time, ordering and regrouping their number sets in a variety of different ways.

As a follow-up activity the children recorded their findings by gluing sets of buttons onto card and writing numbers alongside them.

Modifications and extensions

- The first child 'grabs a group'. Each child estimates the number of objects obtained. The objects are then counted and the nearest estimate(s) earns a point.

    Encourage each child to calculate the difference between their

estimate and the actual number of objects and to make a relevant statement – 'There were seven buttons and my estimate was nine. My estimate was two more than the number of buttons.' Repeat for each child over a number of rounds.
- Each child 'grabs a group' and sorts into twos. If this can be done without leaving a remainder then the child scores a point. Using the same collection of objects, the children sort into threes, fours, fives, and so on, scoring a point each time there is no remainder.

  Encourage children to make relevant statements – 'I had nine buttons and I sorted into four groups of 2 with 1 left over' – and to discuss which types of numbers are good for high scores.

What's the Number?

- You will need a sorting tray, plastic hoop, paper plate or cardboard box, and a collection of objects to sort.
- Prepare a set of cards numbered 1 to 5.
- Shuffle the cards and place them face down on the table.
- The first child takes a card, places it alongside the tray and selects a set of objects corresponding to the number obtained.

  Encourage the child to talk about the objects chosen.
- The second child takes a card and alters the set so that it corresponds to the new number.

  Encourage the child to make a statement concerning the change – 'I've got a 3 so I will have to take out two beads to make my set'.
- The game continues until all the cards have been used.

Modifications and extensions

- Provide each child with a sorting tray. As they draw cards, the children place their sets alongside each other's, comparing and stating differences. Once all the cards have been used the sets can be removed, matched and ordered. Recordings can be made using sticky paper, mosaics, etc. Children can then write appropriate numbers alongside their recordings.
- Include duplicate cards so that the children experience situations in which they do not have to change a set. They do of course have to make an appropriate statement.
- Ask each child to make a set corresponding to a given numeral (say 2). Each child talks about the objects they have used; why

they were selected, their colour, shape, texture, etc. The children are then asked to add *one more* object to their sets. How many now? Which numeral should be displayed now?

Repeat for 'two more', 'one less', 'add three', 'take away one', etc.

Encourage the children to articulate their discoveries.

- Extend the previous version into a game using teacher-prepared flash cards such as:

| more than | | less than |
| take away | | add |

For example,

| 5 | is | 2 | more than | 3 |

The objects may still be used for matching and counting.
- Extend the above activities to include numbers to 10.

Number Dump

- You will need to prepare a set of playing cards showing collections of dots (1 to 6). Alternatively, use cards from a standard pack of playing cards. Provide enough cards to ensure that each player will get at least six.
- Shuffle the cards and deal them out.
- Each child takes a turn rolling a die and 'dumping' cards which correspond to the number obtained. For example, if the die shows 5, then the child could dump the 5 card or the 4 and 1 cards.
- Each child must justify the number(s) dumped by making a statement. For example: 'The die says 5 and I am dumping my 5 card' or 'The die says 5. I can dump my 4 and 1 cards because 4 add 1 is 5.'
- The winner is the first player to dump all cards.

Modifications and extensions

- Use numerals instead of dots and increase the numbers to the range 0–10 or 0–20.

Discussion activities 59

- Instead of a die use a second pack of numbered cards which can be turned over one by one to show what each player has to 'dump'.
- Instead of placing the dots in conventional patterns, place them in irregular positions or within distractors.

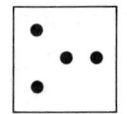

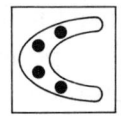

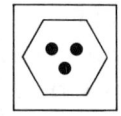

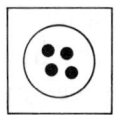

- As well as for playing 'Number Dump', these cards can be used to help with number recognition and conservation. For example, the children could
    - Take turns selecting a card and matching it with its numeral.
    - Sort all the cards into their various sets to investigate which set occurs most/least frequently. The children could then attach a label to each set and order them. (This can be a demanding activity, and can produce some interesting comparative language, particularly if the teacher contrives that there are more 'ones' than 'fives', for instance.)
    - Play 'Snap' with the set of cards.
- Provide a set of pattern cards and a set of numerals.

Each child takes one card from each set and makes a statement relating them. For example, if a child gets

then suitable statements might be 'The set is 3 and the number is 5. 5 is 2 more than 3 so I need 2 more in my set' or 'The set is 2 less than the number so I need to change my 5-card for a 3-card'.

> ## Using the Equaliser Balance
> The equaliser balance is a piece of apparatus found in most primary classrooms. It features in a number of primary schemes such as those of Nuffield Mathematics or the Scottish Primary Mathematics Group, and can be used to help develop number relations by linking with children's experience of using balance scales in weighing activities. When the children hang identical metal rings on equally spaced hooks or (as in this case) place weights in slots, numerical relationships emerge.

Case study

Six middle infants were introduced to the apparatus for the first time. The children began exploring by placing weights on either side of the balance. They agreed that the weights were identical, and that it was their positioning which determined whether they balanced or not. After this initial free-play the teacher posed a challenge.

Teacher: I'm putting a weight in the 5 slot and I want you to use two weights to find a way of balancing it. (7.1)
Victoria: One in the number 1 and one in the 2.
Collette: No, it's not balanced. Move it up one more.
Ryan: Victoria, put the two weights in the number 2.
Teacher: What number has Ryan made?
Craig: Miss, he's made 4 because 2 add 2 makes 4.
Alyson: We need one more to make 5 because Miss put the metal piece in number 5.
Nicola: We need to make it one more because 5 is one more than 4.
Ryan: Take one weight out of the 2, move it up to the 3 because 2 add 3 makes 5.
Teacher: Can anybody think of another way of balancing it with different numbers? (7.4)
Victoria: Miss, one in the 4 and one in the 2, I think.
Teacher: Try it and see if you're right! (7.3)
Ryan: No, Miss, because 4 and 2 is 6 and so I know it's not going to balance. 6 is bigger than 5.
Collette: It's one in the 4 and one in the 1 because 4 and 1 makes 5.
Alyson: 5 is one less than 6.
Craig: Miss, I've got three weights on this side and one weight on this side and it's balanced!
Teacher: Can anyone explain why it has balanced?

Ryan: Well, Miss, there's one in the 5, one in the 3 and one in the 2 on this end.
Craig: 5 and 3 add 2 makes 10.
Victoria: And it's in the 10 on the other side so it's the same number, that's why it's balanced.

Comments

There is obvious similarity between this activity and some of those described in Chapter 1. Notice, however, that these children are not only reinforcing previous ideas but are able to build new ones. In this instance the apparatus also provides a means of testing whether these ideas are correct. A useful strategy, and one that brings this function into play, is to get each child to predict and then use the balance to test their predictions. We see some of this in the above extract when the teacher says, 'Try it and see if you're right' but this could be made a regular feature of the activity achieved by a statement similar to: 'I'm putting a weight in the 6 slot. I want you to think of a way of balancing it with two weights – *don't say anything yet.*' The teacher could then collect together contributions from each child (*without* evaluating them!) before getting the children to test them.

Modification and extensions

- In order to keep the activity going longer, and help the children to build their ideas more fully, it would be a good idea to design a game around it. For example, two dice (numbered 0 to 5) might be rolled and the numbers added to decide where the first weight is to be placed on the balance. The first child then predicts the positions where two further weights would have to be placed to restore equilibrium. The other children accept or challenge the prediction before it is tested. The next child makes a second prediction and the round continues until no one can find a new number combination. The dice are then rolled by the second child and the game continues as before.
- Play a similar game using three (or four) weights to restore equilibrium.

Trio Tricks

- You will need a pack of cards numbered 0 to 10.
- Shuffle the cards and place them face down.
- Each child takes two cards in turn and attempts to make *three* statements relating the numbers obtained. For example, if a child obtains a 2 and a 7 he might offer:

    7 add 2 is 9
    7 subtract 2 is 5
    The difference between 7 and 2 is 5
    7 take away 2 is 5
    7 is 5 more than 2
    2 is 5 less than 7
    2 add 7 is 9

- The remaining children check each statement and a point is awarded if all three relationships are correct.

Modifications and extensions

- Begin with a simpler version in which only one (or two) statements have to be made.
- Play a domino-type game in which each child is provided with a set of cards numbered 1 to 10.

    The first child plays a card and says 'more than' or 'less than'. (If 1 is played then 'more than' must apply; if 10 then 'less than'.) The next child can only play a card if it corresponds to the command *and* he/she can make an appropriate comparative statement. For example,

    The first child plays 4 and says, 'more than'; the second child plays 7 and says, '7 is 3 more than 4'.

    If a child does not have a suitable card, or cannot make an appropriate statement, then he/she misses a turn. The winner is the first child to play all of the cards or the one with the least number of cards remaining.

- Play 'Snap' in which a snap only occurs when the card turned over is 1 more than (or 1 less than) the previous card.

    Vary the rules so that snap corresponds to 'add 2', 'take away 3', etc. Ensure that the child makes a statement justifying the call; 'Snap! 7 take away 3 is 4'. The other children should check, and agree with, the statements made.

- Extend the range of numbers so that it goes from 0 to 20.
- Include duplicate cards.
- Require children to write number statements as well as articulating them. (Teacher-prepared 'flash cards' could be used.)

Arithmogons

This is a popular activity that can work well at a variety of levels.

- You will need to make a board and a set of numbered counters similar to those in Figure 8.1. The board and counters can be made of card and covered with cling-film.

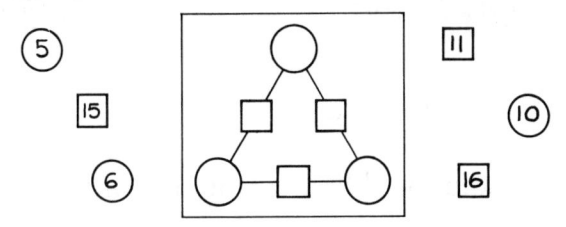

Figure 8.1

- The object of the game is to place the counters on the board so that the sum of the numbers within any two circles is equal to the number in the square which lies between them.

Case study

The session began with the teacher carefully explaining to the children the object of the game. Although they appeared to understand, the children had difficulty articulating what was required.

Gavin: You've got to put 5 up there and if you want to make 15 you've got to put 15 in the middle, then add something on the other circle.

Catherine: Put the numbers in the boxes.

Kimberley: If you want to make 11 you put 10 there and 1 there in the circles.

Mathew: If you want to make 16 add 10 and put 6 in the middle – no, put 16 in the middle, 10 in the one circle and 6 in the other circle.

The children then worked together placing the circular counters and adding numbers to arrive at a solution (see Figure 8.2a).

Teacher: Do you think there is another way that we can put these numbers on the board to get a solution? [*The board is cleared and Kimberley volunteers to start. She puts the 11 in one of the square boxes.*]

Mathew: She's put 11 in first – we must put the circles in now to add them up.

Catherine: This is a different problem now. [*The children continue taking turns and arrive at what they consider to be a different solution (Figure 8.2b).*]

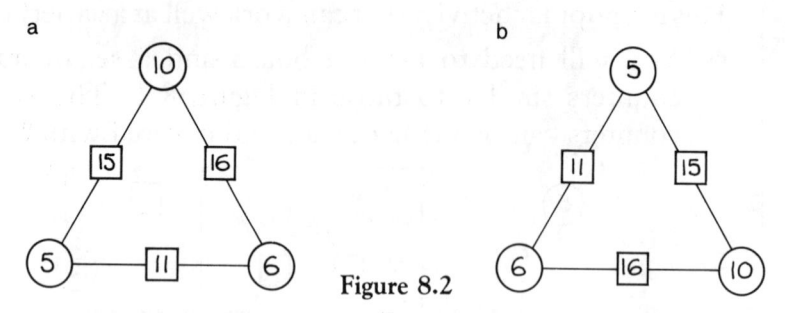

Figure 8.2

Teacher: Is this solution different from the one we did earlier?

All: Yes.

Gavin: It's quite different.

Mathew: The 11 is up there, and the other 11 is down the bottom. But the 11 is supposed to be next to the 15 and the 10 is not supposed to be at the top!

Teacher: So there's more than one way of getting a solution?

All: Yes.

Notice that in fact the two representations illustrated in Figure 8.2 are equivalent (one is merely a rotation of the other). It is the method of solution that differs.

Having allowed the children to negotiate their understanding of the problem in a closed situation, the teacher then decided to open it up. Each child was given a teacher-prepared worksheet which depicted the board and asked to insert their own numbers according to the earlier rules. (This strategy frees children to attain at whatever level they are able, and removes any constraints which may otherwise have been imposed by a teacher's own expectations.) The children were also told they should think carefully about what they were doing as they would be required to talk about their work afterwards. (7.5) The children were then left to complete this work while the teacher moved on to work with another group.

Comments

It can be useful to use a relatively closed situation to introduce new ideas. The experience that the children gained by placing the numbered counters on the board was quickly assimilated and transferred to the worksheet activity. An intermediate stage could be introduced if necessary, in which the children are given blank counters on which to write their own numbers. These counters could then be placed on the board and moved around to find a solution.

When the teacher rejoined the group each child talked about what they had done. For example:

Gavin: I wanted to make 9 so I put 9 at the top and 9 in the middle square. Then I put 0 at the bottom. I wanted to make 1 so I put 0, 1, 1. To make 10 I added 9 and 1 [Figure 8.3a].
Teacher: Tell us about the bottom one [Figure 8.3b].
Gavin: 90 at the top. I wanted to make 100 so I put 10 down the bottom and 100 in the square. Then I . . .

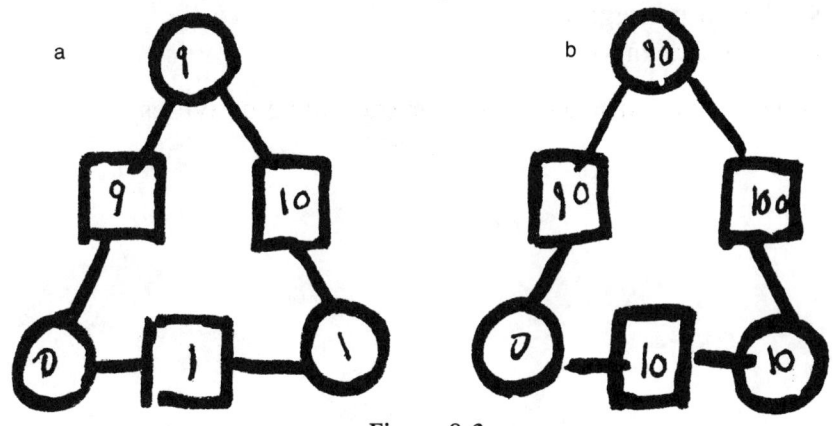

Figure 8.3

Gavin's work with multiples of 10 and with numbers 'around 10' and 'around 100' is interesting. The group had not been introduced formally to place value, and the intuitive development on Gavin's part seems to be in line with findings reported by the PrIME project (1987, p. 14). In that particular instance children were asked to draw a square, write any number inside it, and then put a number at each of its four corners so that they added up to the first number. Examples of work received from top infants indicate an appreciation of place value and negative numbers which 'seem to have developed from calculator use without formal teaching of the topic'.

Modifications and extensions

- If necessary begin with a simpler version such as:

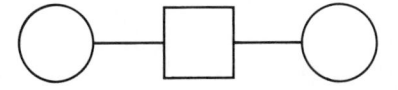

- Change the operation to multiplication, with the numbers in the squares being found by multiplying numbers in circles. Subtraction or division could also be used but it will be necessary to discuss how the operation should be applied since $15 - 8 \neq 8 - 15$.
- Use arithmogons in the context of money. Initially coins could be placed on the board; later numbers could be written in pence; even later numbers could be written using decimal notation.
- Present similar activities developing the idea reported by PrIME:
  - Draw a triangle and place any number inside. Write a number at each vertex so that their sum is equal to the first number.
  - Use a square.
  - Use a pentagon.
  - Use a hexagon.
- Have a calculator available for the above activities.

Star Number 1

This is an extension of 'Arithmogons'.

- Challenge the children to find numbers such that:
    1. the sum of the numbers within any two circles is equal to the number in the square which lies between them, and
    2. the 'star number' is the sum of the three numbers written in the squares (Figure 8.4).

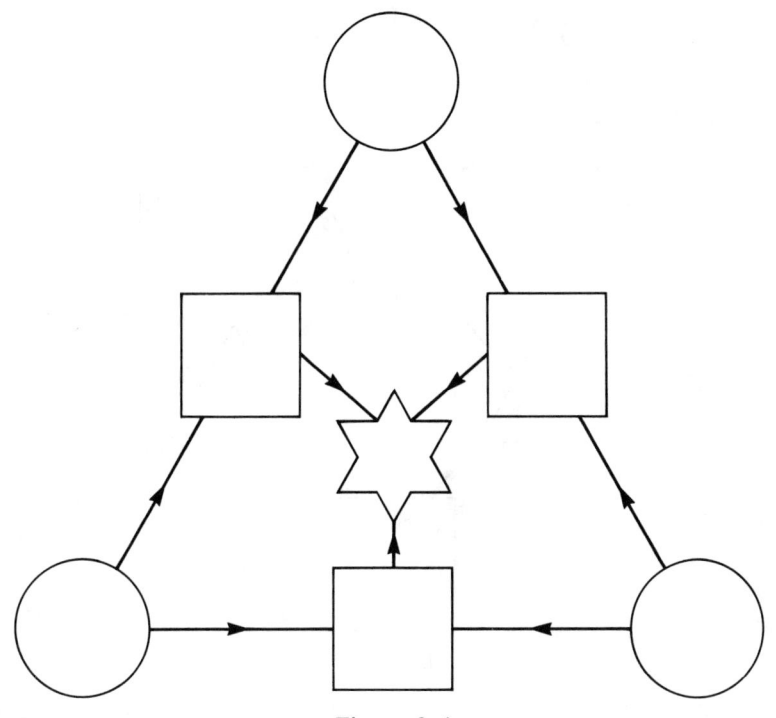

Figure 8.4

- Encourage the children to investigate whether the star number is related to the three numbers in the circles.

Star Number 2

This is a further extension of 'Arithmogons'.

- After adding the circle numbers to produce 'square' numbers, the square numbers are added to produce numbers for the triangles. These are then added to produce the star number (Figure 8.5).

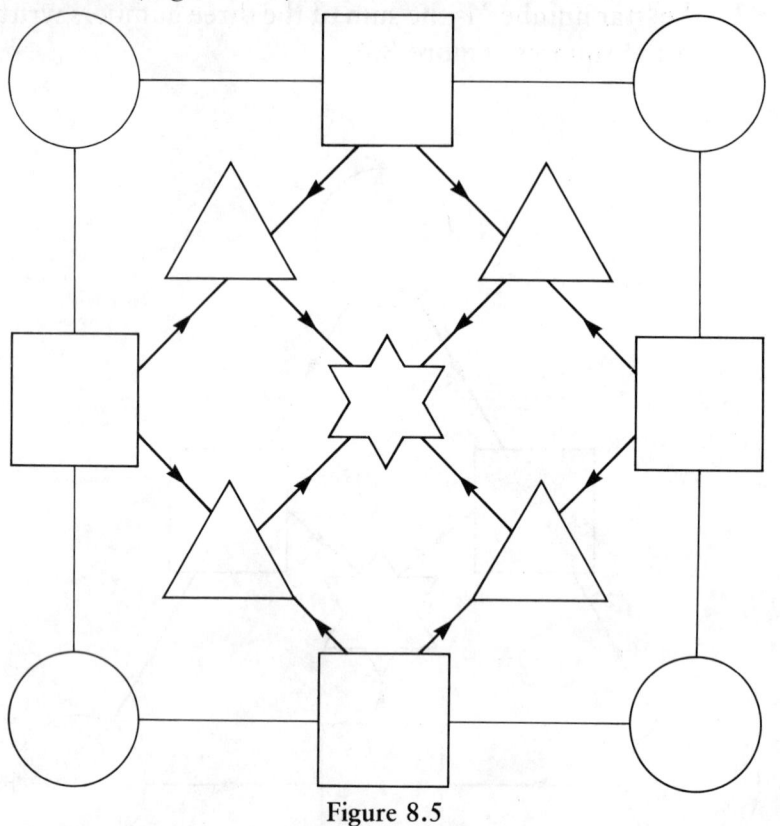

Figure 8.5

- Again, encourage children to seek relationships between the various numbers.
- Challenge children to produce their own extensions.

3, 5, 7

- Using just the numbers 3, 5, 7 and the operators + and − as many times as they wish, challenge the children to make all the whole numbers from 1 to 10.
- There should be a variety of different ideas in evidence. For example,

    7 − 3 − 3 = 1
    5 + 3 − 7 = 1
    5 + 5 + 5 − 7 − 7 = 1

- To encourage the sharing of these different ideas, make the activity into a game.

    Player A takes a turn stating and writing a method of making the number 1; player B then attempts to find a different method, as does player C, player D, and so on. The children's ideas can be recorded on a large sheet of paper.

    When no alternative methods can be found, it is player B's turn to start a new round with a 'target' of the number 2.

- If the children are unable to find alternatives and you want to continue with the investigation, it might be profitable to ask a helpful question. For example, 'We've all been using three numbers, could we do it with four or five?'
- Alternatively, you may want to be more direct and provide an example of your own to move the activity forward – 'I can think of one using five numbers... Can anyone find others?'
- When the children have made all the numbers from 1 to 10 you might ask whether they think they can produce all the numbers to 20 or 100 and to give their reasons for thinking so.

Modifications and extensions

- Roll three dice. Using the numbers obtained, along with the + and − operators, make as many numbers as possible.

    Again, this can develop into a self-supporting activity in which each child takes a turn, makes a move, and states (as well as writes) a suitable result.
- Other rules can be introduced. For example, all numbers have to be used or the operators can only be used a maximum of twice each.
- Allow children to use other operators (×, ÷).

- Use a calculator; only the 3, 5, 7, +, − keys are to be used.
- Play 'What's the Question?'. Give an answer and ask children to decide on possible questions that might have been asked. (For example, if the answer is '8' then possible suggestions might be '9 − 1', '4 + 3 + 1', '16/2' or '2 × 4'.

Again, the children's ideas could be recorded and compared using a large sheet of paper and 'rules' or restrictions made as appropriate.

Boxes

- This game is played by two children.
- Each child requires a pack of cards numbered 0 to 9 and two flash cards:

    | is greater than | | is less than |

- The object of the game is to make correct number statements of the form 'A B is greater than C D'. For example,

    | 5 | 3 | | is greater than | | 4 | 9 |

- Shuffle each pack of cards and place them face down in front of the players.
- Player 1 takes a card and places it face up in position A, B, C or D. Once the card is placed it *cannot be moved*.
- Player 1 draws three further cards, *one at a time*, and places them in any of the vacant positions. (Again, once placed, cards cannot be moved.)
- If a correct statement is realised on the playing of the fourth and final card, then the player scores the number of points indicated by the card in position C. Incorrect statements do not score.
- Player 2 then takes a turn. (If preferred, each player can take one card at a time and place their cards alternatively.)
- The game continues into a second round with each player attempting to make statements of the type: 'A B is less than C D'.
- Correct statements earn the number of points shown by the card in position A.
- The game is played over an even number of rounds and the winner is the player with most points.

Modifications and extensions

- Begin with a simpler version involving one-digit numbers.

  | A | is greater than | B |

  | A | is less than | B |

- Extend the game to a three-digit version.

  | A | B | C | is greater than | D | E | F |

  Ensure that players make a statement when placing numbers. For example, 'I've got a 7. I'm putting it here [A] so it stands for 7 thousand'.
- Play the game with two teams. Encourage teams to discuss the best position for a number before placing it. Ask the children why the scoring system is different for 'greater than' and 'less than'.
- Use packs of cards with duplicate numbers.
- Instead of cards use two dice (or spinners) numbered 0 to 5. To generate a number the player rolls both dice and adds *or* subtracts the numbers to obtain a value between 0 and 9. He/she then places this value in one of the vacant positions A, B, C, or D.
- Players roll two dice and generate numbers between 0 and 9 in whatever way they choose. For example, suppose 3 and 4 are obtained on the dice. Then

  $$3 + 4 = 7$$
  $$4 - 3 = 1$$
  $$3 \times 4 = 12; \quad 1 + 2 = 3$$
  $$4 \div 3 = 1 \text{ remainder } 1; \quad 1 + 1 = 2$$

  or even

  $$3 + 4 + 3 + 4 = 14; \quad 1 + 4 = 5!$$

Across the River

- To make this problem attractive to young children provide Playmobil people and a toy boat. Alternatively, use counters to represent people (any number may be used) and make a drawing of the boat.
- The people want to cross the river. A sailor offers to take them in his boat but the boat can only carry three people at once. How many trips are needed?

Setting the scene

This group of four middle infants met this problem for the first time. However, they were experienced problem-solvers and had worked cooperatively on previous occasions.

After posing the problem, the teacher encouraged each child to predict the number of trips required. There were eight people and the children's predictions were four, three, three, and seven trips!

Teacher: Well, we've got three different ideas. Can anyone explain their reasons?
Ceri: Three trips because there are eight people.
Daniel: Two can go, and there are one–two, three–four, five–six, seven–eight [*puts the people into groups of two as he counts*].
Teacher: Why have you grouped them, Daniel? (7.6)
Daniel: Because they can fit into the boat; sets of two.
Ceri: I think three trips.
Teacher: Why? Can you show us?
Ceri: Put one in the boat [*puts one passenger in the boat with the sailor*]. Put one more in [*he does*], and one more in [*he does*].
Teacher: Oh ... I think we have a problem. Look, the boat is sinking! The boat can only carry three people. How many have we got in the boat?
Ceri: Three.
Ben: No, there's four with the sailor!

Comments

The teacher allowed the children to negotiate their own understanding of the problem and its solution. She anticipated that there would be difficulties concerning the inclusion of the sailor, but was careful to allow the children to resolve this matter for themselves.

Notice that Daniel grouped the eight people into sets of two and was thus able to justify that four trips would be necessary. However, since the children had no formal experience of division they were not able to articulate an explanation in terms of 'eight divided by two gives four'. Later, when the children went on to consider the number of trips necessary for six people and then ten people to cross the river, they became very excited by the discovery of a pattern, which Daniel described as

> Four and four is eight.
> Three and three is six.
> Five and five is ten.

Ceri was able to extend this to 'six and six is twelve' and use this result to predict correctly the number of trips (six) required when twelve people wish to cross the river.

During this activity the children engaged in the processes of *specialising* (exploring particular cases), *pattern seeking*, *predicting*, and *testing*. Indeed, they arrived at a generalisation, namely that if there are an even number (n) of people waiting to cross the river, then $n/2$ trips will be necessary. Although they were not able to state the generalisation in this way, nor to provide an explanation of their solution (that there are $n/2$ groups of 2), they had discovered a method (based on their experience of addition) which would allow them to solve any similar problem.

This process-based approach is at the heart of problem solving and investigating. Further experiences in which an odd number of people cross the river, or in which the boat carries groups of three, four, or more passengers, will lead the children towards further generalisations and a growing awareness of the underlying explanation.

Modifications and extensions

- Investigate using an odd number of people. For five people three trips are required, but there will only be one person on one of these. (This might be the first, second or third trip – discuss this point with the children.)
- What would happen if the boat could carry three passengers? What about four or five?
- Consider similar situations in different contexts.

    For example, if a taxi can carry a total of five people then how many taxis will be required to transport seventeen passengers? How many will travel in each taxi and how many spare seats will there be? Is there more than one way of grouping the people into the taxis?
- Consider eggs in egg-boxes. How many egg-boxes will be needed for twenty-six eggs? How many spaces will there be left for additional eggs?
- Discuss similar situations in terms of money. If cinema tickets cost £3, then how many can be bought with £14? How much money is left? How much more will be needed to buy five tickets?

74 Resource pack

Algebra

Attainment Target 5 – Pupils should recognise and use patterns, relationships and sequences and make generalisations

Caterpillars	page 74
Different Ways	76
Dominoes	77
Number Frames	79

Attainment Target 6 – Pupils should recognise and use functions, formulae, equations and inequalities

Make Fifteen	page 82
Function Machines	84

Caterpillars

- You will need threading beads of different colours, sizes and shapes; laces; and cards numbered 1 to 6.
- Working in pairs the children select two cards and make a caterpillar that matches the pattern of the numbers obtained. For example, if 2 and 3 are chosen, then they have to thread a 2, 3 pattern (Figure 8.6).

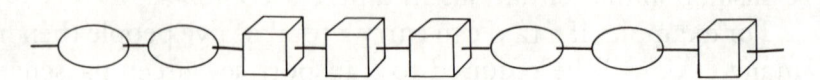

Figure 8.6

Case study

The teacher worked with four children, Jodi, Leon, Aimee, and Michelle. This was the first time they had attempted the activity although all the children had had experience of threading beads during free-play situations.

[Each child selects a card and makes a statement identifying the number obtained. Jodi has a 6 and threads six round red beads onto a lace. Her partner, Leon, has a 2 and he adds two identical beads to the lace.]

Teacher: Does this show the pattern of 6 and 2?
Aimee: It looks like one, two, three ... eight.

Teacher: Yes, there are eight beads now and they are all red and round. Has anyone any ideas about what we might do to show that there was a 6 and a 2? (7.7)

Michelle: Change the colour of the 2 ...

Leon: ... or change the shape. [*Replaces the two red beads with two blue beads.*]

Teacher: What would you thread now, Aimee, to show the 6, 2 pattern? [*Aimee chooses six round yellow beads.*] Has Aimee kept to the pattern? [*All the children agree that she has: six red, two blue, six yellow.*] What do you think we ought to thread now?

Michelle: Two blue.

Teacher: Are you all happy with that?

Comments

It is interesting that the children were all prepared to accept six red, two blue, six yellow. The teacher decided to accept this also – number was the key characteristic at this stage, and later discussion could involve the attributes of colour and shape.

The children continued Jodi and Leon's pattern further before the teacher turned the group's attention to Michelle and Aimee's numbers. The children were then left to continue with the activity in pairs while the teacher joined another group.

Modifications and extensions

- Make cards which specify colour and shape as well as number. This can be done by drawing and colouring if children are unable to recognise words.
- Use other materials such as pegs and pegboard, Unifix, or Multi-link instead of beads.
- Have the children take turns threading/spotting patterns.
- Have the children work in threes and extend to number patterns such as 3, 2, 4, 3, 2, 4, 3, 2, 4, ...

Different Ways

... of giving five sweets to two children.

- Each child in the group makes a suggestion which can be compared and checked using counters, blocks, or real sweets!
- What about six sweets? Seven (or more) sweets?
- What happens if there are three children?
- Make the activity into a game by producing two packs of cards. One pack could depict various quantities of sweets, while the second could show various groups of children.

  The first child selects a card from each pack and suggests a way in which the sweets might be distributed. For example, the child might say, 'There are four sweets and two children. Each child can have two sweets'. The group checks the statement and if it is correct the first child scores a point.

  The second child then attempts to make a different statement concerning the first pair of cards.

  The round continues with each child attempting to make further statements concerning the cards. When no new relationships can be found the round ends. The second child selects two further cards and a new round begins.

Modifications and extensions

- Change the context – for example, to 'Different ways of putting five spots on the ladybird's wings'. Use black counters and provide each child with a card showing a picture of a ladybird.

  Encourage the children to produce different arrangements and compare them.

  Extend to six or more spots.

  Increase the number of ladybirds.
- Adapt the above ideas to match the theme you are currently using in your classroom.
- Consider the various ways of placing eggs in an egg-box. For example,

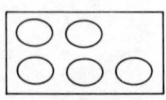

could be perceived as 2 + 3 or 2 + 2 + 1 or 4 + 1 or ... while

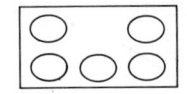

might be described as 2 + 1 + 2 or 1 + 1 + 1 = 3 or ...
- Using coins find different ways of making 5p, 6p, 10p, 20p, etc.
- Thread beads onto laces to show different number combinations of 5 or 6, etc.
- Use straws to partition sets of objects placed on paper plates.

Dominoes
- You will require a set of dominoes and some sorting hoops.
- Have the children sort the dominoes into sets of their choosing.

Case Study

This group of 6-year-olds decided to sort the dominoes into 'even totals' and 'odd totals', a Level 2 activity. They agreed that zero should be treated as an even number, then they quickly completed the activity demonstrating good group cooperation and mental facility.

The teacher decided to encourage the children to extend their investigation further.

Teacher: What do you notice about the two sets that we have made?
Luke: There are more dominoes in the even set.
Hannah: All the doubles are in the even set.
Teacher: That's interesting, Hannah.
Claire: There's twelve odd totals ... and ...
Teacher: How many even totals?
Children [counting together]: ... Sixteen!
Gavin: If you've got an even number and an odd number it goes in the odd set.
Luke: Two odd numbers like 3 and 5 make an even.
Gareth: Let's sort the dominoes into two even; two odd; one even; one odd. [*The children overlap their hoops and produce the arrangement shown in Figure 8.7.*]
Claire: All the odd numbers have got even totals and all the even numbers have got even totals.
Gareth: And all the odd and even numbers have got odd totals.

                    Two even   One even, one odd   Two odd
                                          Figure 8.7

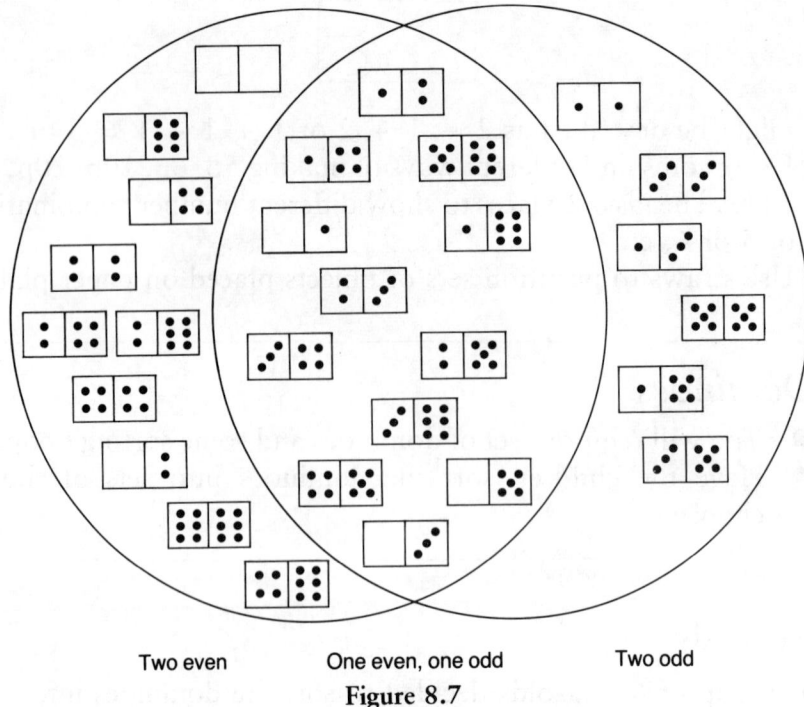

Comments

Sorting a set of dominoes can provide a rich source of number experience for young children. Encourage the children to sort in as many different ways as possible: odd or even, totals of 7, differences of 2, dominoes which exhibit 'one more than' or 'one less than' property, and so on.

Once the blocks are sorted, encourage the children to make generalised statements about their sets. It is interesting to note, in the previous case study, that Claire is able to move towards such a generalisation (a Level 4 skill) with her observation that 'All the odd numbers have got even totals'. This statement needs some refinement ('Any two odd numbers added together produce an even number') which might be achieved by asking the group a 'What if . . . ?' type of question ('What if we have three odd numbers?').

Don't restrict the sorting to Venn diagrams. Placing the blocks in a matrix can reveal many interesting patterns. See how many patterns and sets you can find!

Modifications and extensions

- A standard set of dominoes (a 'double 6' set) has 28 blocks. Challenge children to determine the number of blocks in a double 5 or a double 9 set. How are the number of dominoes in different sets related?

Discussion activities 79

Encourage children to make, and sort, various sets of dominoes.
- What sets can be produced if the children are allowed to write three numbers on a block (Figure 8.8)?

Figure 8.8

> ## Number Frames
> - You will need a '100-square' for each pair of children.
>   Using stiff card prepare a 3 × 3 frame which exactly covers nine of the numbers on the 100-square. The centre section of the frame should be cut out so that when it is placed on the 100-square the centre number can be seen. 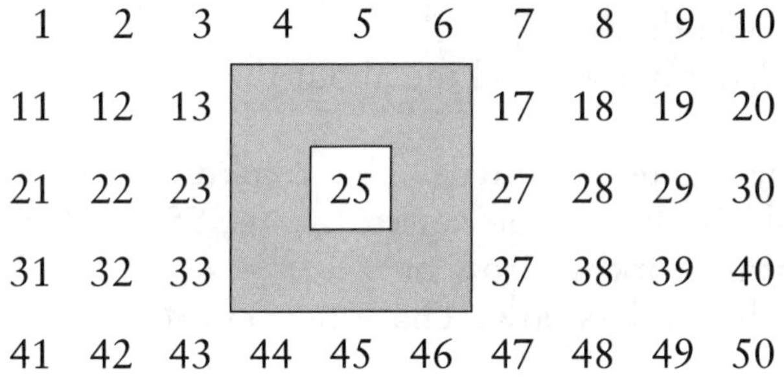
>
> ```
>  1  2  3  4  5  6  7  8  9 10
> 11 12 13           17 18 19 20
> 21 22 23      25   27 28 29 30
> 31 32 33           37 38 39 40
> 41 42 43 44 45 46 47 48 49 50
> ```
>
> - The children place the frame in various positions on the 100-square and attempt to identify the unseen numbers.

Case study

This group of eight top infants worked in pairs. Each child took a turn placing the frame on the 100-square. The children then attempted to identify the missing numbers and record the pattern on a worksheet which the teacher provided. The teacher joined the group to find out what progress has been made.

Teacher: Let's all have a look at what Sacha and Charlene have been doing. (7.2)

Sacha: We chose 27 in the middle. We started to fill in but then we got stuck and ...

Charlene: ... then we found 16 because it comes after 15 and we just filled in the other numbers.

[*The teacher gets each pair of children to talk about their work before posing a new challenge.*]

Teacher: Is there anything you notice about the numbers in your squares?

Christopher: They're not in order.

Teacher: What do you mean, Christopher?

Christopher: Well, there are some numbers missing. See – 1, 2, 3 then 11, 12, 13, so there's lots missing like 4, 5, 6, 7, 8, 9, 10.

Sacha [*reading down in rhythm*]: 16 ... 26 ... 36

Dawn: Miss, they're going across in ones but going down in tens.

Christopher: I did this one without using the frame or the 100-square. [*Christopher has opened up a new situation. It is much more difficult to carry out the activity without the help of the square and frame. Dawn decides to have a go and writes 45 in the middle of her worksheet.*]

Dawn: It's easy to work out the middle one – 44, 45, 46 – but how do you do the top?

Teacher: What did you tell me about the numbers going down? (7.7)

Dawn: They go down in tens. This is hard. 44 and 10 is ... I'm going to look at the square ... 54, 55, 56. Oh, now we've got to work this row out.

Jaqueline: It's 10 less now. That's 34, 35, 36.

Comments

Notice that Dawn was prepared to attempt to predict the number pattern without the help of the 100-square. Initially it was necessary for her to refer back to the 100-square to identify the necessary numbers, but she and the other children were soon able to work without this aid.

During the latter part of the session the children worked in pairs setting a challenge for their partner by writing a number in the centre of the worksheet. *After* predicting the pattern the 100-square was used to check the result.

Modifications and extensions

- Use different-shaped frames which allow two or more central numbers to be seen.
- Cut the 'hole' in varying positions on the frame.
- Instead of using a 100-square, arrange the numbers in columns of eight (or six, or twelve, etc.).
- Encourage the children to look for patterns within their squares. For example,

13	14	15
23	24	25
33	34	35

14 + 34 = 23 + 25
13 + 35 = 15 + 33

Do these results hold for all 'squares'? Why?
There are opportunities here to discuss methods of performing mental calculations.

$$13 + 35 = 10 + 3 + 30 + 5$$
$$= 10 + 30 + 3 + 5 = 40 + 8 = 48$$

Calculators could be used to extend the pattern and/or check results.

- An alternative to using frames is to draw letters and shapes on the 100-square.

13	14	15
23	24	25
33	34	35

13	14	15
23	24	25
33	34	35

13	14	15
23	24	25
33	34	35

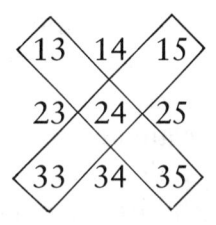

The children can be encouraged to investigate the number patterns within the shapes.

- Instead of using the 1, 2, 3 ... sequence, try 2, 4, 6 ..., 3, 6, 9 ..., 1, 5, 9, 13, ... etc.

```
        3   6   9  12  15  18
       21  24              36
       39  42      48      54
       57  60              72
       75  78  81  84  87  90
       93  96  99 102 105 108
```

- Encourage children to experiment and set similar problems for one another.
- The computer program Ergo, which was supplied to all primary schools by MEP as part of the Micro Primer Pack, provides other investigations into number patterns.

Make Fifteen

- Prepare two sets of playing cards numbered 0 to 10.
- Provide apparatus (such as blocks or counters) for counting and/or checking.
- Place the two sets of cards face down on the table. The children take turns selecting a card from each pack, totalling the numbers obtained, and deciding what needs to be done in order to obtain a final score of 15. For example, if 6 and 7 are chosen then 2 must be added; if 10 and 6 are chosen then 1 must be subtracted.

Case study

The teacher used the activity to assess the strategies that a particular group of middle infants applied when faced with addition and subtraction situations. The teacher focused attention on each child in turn, and some of the questioning is quite direct as she seeks to evaluate the children's levels of understanding.

The counting apparatus is particularly useful; it allows the children to demonstrate their methods as well as providing a source of support.

Nadine [selecting a 5 and a 4]: 6.
Teacher: Nadine, can you explain how you got 6? (7.6)
Nadine [holding up her hands]: 9 ... [*then counting on her fingers*] ... 10, 11, 12, 13, 14, 15 – that's 6!
Teacher: You started from 9, Nadine – why?
Nadine: 5 and 4 is 9.
Teacher: Can you show us how you would do this with the cubes? [*Nadine takes fifteen cubes to explain that she grouped them as 5, 4 and 6. Alun takes a 2 and a 4. He says, '6', but seems unsure about what to do next.*] How do you get to 15, Alun? Do you need more cubes?
Alun: Yes.
Teacher: How many more? [*Alun takes a handful of cubes and counts them. He has collected another seven and he puts them with the original six. He then takes two more.*]
Nadine: I had a 9 and I needed 6, and Alun had 6 and he needed a 9! [*Alun has another turn. He takes 4 and 3 and says, '7'. He slowly counts out another eight cubes and checks that he*

has fifteen. Sam selects 9 and 2. He takes the cubes, counts eleven and then stops.]
Sam: Four ... no, two.
Teacher: You need two more do you, Sam?
Sam: I need two and another two.
[Leon takes 12 and 6. He counts out twelve cubes, then adds another six, then discards three.]
Teacher: What was different about Leon's score?
Nadine: He had too many.
Teacher: How many did you put back, Leon?
Leon: Three!

Modifications and extensions

- Play a simpler game first using one pack of cards. Each child selects a card and says what has to be done to 'Make 10'. Follow up this activity with consolidation exercises of the type

$$3 + \boxed{} = 10$$

and

$$\boxed{} + 4 = 10$$

- Change the target number. For example, if you are using one pack of cards try 5 or 12; with two packs try 11 or 17.
- Play a similar game using three packs of cards and appropriate target numbers.
- Extend this activity into a self-supporting activity in which children attempt to make a given target number in as many ways as possible.

  Suppose the target number is 15. The first child scores a point by stating (and writing) a number statement linking any three numbers with an answer of 15. For example,

$$6 + 11 - 2 = 15$$

or

$$4 + 5 + 6 = 15$$

It is then the second child's turn to make a different number statement with an answer of 15. The game continues with children taking turns and checking one another's statements until no one can find a new number combination. The target number can then be changed.

84 *Resource pack*

Extra rules can be imposed as desired. For example, only the addition operation might be allowed, or perhaps only three numbers between 0 and 20 could be used. The children will probably have their own ideas about the rules they want to make, so be flexible.

Function Machines

- The purpose of this Level 3 activity is to encourage children to think of number operations in terms of

    INPUT → PROCESS → OUTPUT

    Thus, if the process is 'add 2', then an input of 3 produces an output of 5:

    $$3 \to 5$$
    $$7 \to 9$$
    $$9 \to 11 \quad \text{etc.}$$

- It is useful to provide a large piece of card showing a function machine (Figure 8.9a), a set of numbered cards, and a collection of operation cards (Figure 8.9b).

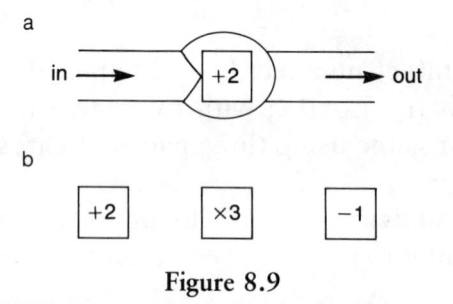

    a

    in → [+2] → out

    b

    [+2] [×3] [−1]

    Figure 8.9

Case study

This group of six top infants had met the idea of a function machine previously and worked with machines which process attribute blocks (see Modifications and extensions, page 86).

The teacher introduced the activity by asking the group whether it might be possible to make a machine which 'changes numbers'.

Mathew: I don't know what you mean.
Catherine: Well, you just say 1 in and 3 comes out.
Mathew: Yes, 1 could go in and 3 come out.
Victoria: It would make 1 into 3!
Teacher: How do you think it could make 1 into 3?
Victoria: Adding 2?

Mathew: There could be a little man in there with a rubber and a pencil. He could change it from 1 to 3.

[*At this point the teacher introduces the card showing a function machine, the number cards, and the operation cards. The children investigate using the operation + 2.*]

Kimberley: It's like a sum now. You've added 1 to 2 and made 3.

Lisa: It's an adding machine and it adds 2.

Catherine: What if you have 3 add 2 is 5, and 5 add 2 is 7, and 7 add 2 is 9, ...

Victoria: Well, it's not the two times table is it?

Lisa: They're odd numbers; we've done 'odds and evens' before.

Gavin: 2 add 2 is 4, and if 4 goes in then 6 will come out, and 6 will make an 8 ... that's like the two times table!

Teacher: If these have been 'adding machines' can you think of any other sorts of machines? (7.4)

Mathew: Multiplying, times.

Catherine: Taking aways.

Comments

During the discussion the children were keen to re-introduce the outputs back into the machine and search for pattern (see Gavin's comment, '2 add 2 is 4, and if 4 goes in then 6 will come out ...'). The teacher decided to exploit this and quickly drew up a worksheet showing a series of machines linked together.

After further group activity which involved writing numbers onto the machines, each child was given a worksheet and asked to develop a similar idea of his/her own. The children were told they would be expected to explain what they had done in due course. When the teacher rejoined the group some ten minutes later, there were some interesting developments.

Catherine: I multiplied 3 by 3 and got 9. Then by 3 again and got 27. But I can't go any further.

Lisa: You can use your calculator.

Catherine [*using the calculator*]: 81 ... 243 ... 729.

Gavin: That's ridiculous. You can't get huge numbers like that. You've only done 1, 2, 3, 4, 5, 6 times 3.

Kimberley: Yes, it's too much. Let me show you. [*Kimberley and Gavin work through, checking Catherine's answers.*]

Gavin: Well, that's amazing!

Lisa: Well, I did taking away and I got down to 1 so I changed to adding up and the numbers got bigger.

Gavin: You haven't seen mine. I've written mine like a calculator because you can go on and on!

Modifications and extensions

- Investigate inputs and outputs with single function machines; produce worksheets for recording and consolidation.
- Varying the operation used (+ 2, − 3, × 3, etc.) can produce a multitude of possibilities. Try using other forms also, such as 'half of', 'quarter of', 'double and add 1', etc.
- Discuss what happens when the function machine is reversed. For example, with the + 2 machine we have

  $$1 \to 3, \quad 3 \to 5, \quad 5 \to 7$$

  If the machine is 'reversed'

  $$3 \to 1, \quad 5 \to 3, \quad 7 \to 5$$

  What is the operation? Consider various cases.
- Encourage children to devise their own function machines for processing numbers.

  Develop this into an activity in which one child produces a list of inputs/outputs and the other children have to guess the operation. For example,

  $$2 \to 4, \quad 3 \to 9, \quad 4 \to 16, \ldots$$

  The children suggest possible operations after each input/output is given. If a child guesses correctly after the first piece of information is given, then 5 points are scored; after the second piece of information 4 points, and so on.
- Challenge the children to produce a series of linked machines in which the number going in is the same as the number coming out. One possibility is by using the operations + 1, − 1, × 2, ÷ 2.

  Vary the number of links used.

  Vary the challenge, say to make a machine where the number coming out is twice (three times, half, ...) the number going in.

  Encourage children to set similar tasks for each other.
- Use similar ideas with a set of attribute blocks. The operations would now involve changing colour, shape, size or thickness. For example, a machine could be devised to change a large, thin, red circle into a small, thick, red circle. Experiment with single and linked machines using a variety of operations.

Measures

Attainment Target 8 – Pupils should estimate and measure quantities, and appreciate the approximate nature of measurement

Tall, Taller, Tallest   page 87
Make an Orange   89
Houses of Hamlyn   90

Tall, Taller, Tallest

- You will need a collection of soft toys or dolls of various sizes.
- If you structure your collection thoughtfully then this will encourage much comparative language.

Case study

In this particular case the class teacher had collected together a set of twenty-seven knitted teddy bears. These bears had been made by parents as a home–school task. The teacher had been specific in requesting that each parent should make a particular type of teddy. This meant that teddies were available in three sizes, each with three different lengths of scarf, and three different types of filling, which resulted in bears of various weights.

In this Level 1 activity the teacher worked with a group of five very young reception class children. She was looking to develop ideas of sameness and difference, to encourage the children to begin sorting and classifying, and to promote comparative language.

The activity took place early in the school year and the teacher was prepared to accept what the children had to offer and allow ideas and language to grow over a period of time.

Teacher: Right, we've got a lot of lovely teddy bears. Leanne, can you find me a teddy that looks the same as this one?
Leanne: That one.
Teacher: Pick it up and show everyone. Do you all think it looks the same?
All: Yes.
Teacher: What do you think is the same about them?   (7.1)
Laura: Because the two are little.
Teacher: They are little. What else is the same?
Richard: They are the same colour.

Craig: They've both got arms and legs!
Richard [*pointing to a larger teddy*]: That's a big one.
Teacher: Yes, let's stand them up together. This one is short and that one is tall.
Marc: That's a big one over there.
Teacher [*standing up the tallest teddy*]: Yes, that one is short, that one is tall, but this one is even taller. He's the tallest. What else can you tell me about the teddies?
Leanne: That's little and that's big. That's a little scarf and that's a big one.
Teacher: Yes, this scarf is longer than that scarf.
Marc: That teddy goes with that one because they are both big.
Craig: This one is the littlest.
Teacher: Yes, he's the shortest.
Richard: And this one is the tallest!

Comments

The session continued with the children matching pairs of teddies according to their heights. This activity had been prompted by Marc's earlier suggestion that two teddies should go together 'because they are both big'. The children recorded the relationship by linking bears together with straws, while the teacher stressed the vocabulary 'is as tall as', 'is the same height as', 'is as short as'. Many similar sessions in which children match and sort the teddies will be needed to develop fully the children's language and conceptual understanding.

Modifications and extensions

- Use comparative language

    tall, taller, tallest,
    short, shorter, shortest

    in a variety of other contexts (especially with reference to the children themselves).
- Use Venn diagrams and Carroll diagrams to carry out sorting activities.
- Have matching and sorting activities in which attention is focused on the lengths of the scarves and the weights of the teddy bears, with extensions as discussed above.
- Investigate the relationship between height and weight. If teddy is the tallest does that mean he's the heaviest? What about the children themselves in this respect?

Make an Orange

- You will need Cuisenaire rods.
- Give each child an orange rod and ask them to make equivalent lengths using the other colours.
- Encourage the children to compare their results by placing various combinations of colours alongside each other.
- This can be made into a self-supporting activity in which each child takes a turn placing a 'new' combination of rods alongside those previously constructed.
- Ensure that the children make a statement describing the cases they discover. For example, 'A long blue with a white is the same length as an orange' or 'I've made an orange rod with a light green, a dark green and a white.'
- The children can record their work by drawing around the rods and colouring.

Modifications and extensions

- Use a different colour rod as your starting point.
- If a white rod is a 'one-rod' and a red rod is a 'two-rod', what is the value of a light green rod? Find the value of all other rods. What if the red rod is the one-rod?
- Turn the last activity around by asking the children to make a five-rod or a seven-rod.
- Use Cuisenaire rods as arbitrary units of length in a variety of contexts.

    One group of reception class children were using the rods to measure the height of a toy teddy bear. They began by lying a teddy on the table and placing a row of red rods alongside it.

Andrew: 1, 2, 3, 4, 5, 6, 7. We've put out seven red rods.
Jamie: That's taller – Teddy is shorter.
Simon: Take one away – there's six now.
Teacher: Do you think Teddy is six rods tall?
Andrew: That doesn't look right. Teddy isn't tall enough for seven, but that's not right. Seven is too many and six is not enough.
Jamie: He's somewhere between six and seven.
[*The children then used the various other colour combinations of rods in an attempt to measure the teddy more accurately. Chris and Andrew used the shortest, white rods.*]

Andrew: Look, thirteen little cubes!
Chris: I think that's right because they are little. I think the blocks should be smaller because it's easier.

> ## Houses of Hamlyn
> - This activity was planned as part of the class's theme on the Pied Piper of Hamlyn.
> - Over a period of time the children had constructed a three-dimensional model of the main street of Hamlyn. The street contained ten houses made from different-sized cardboard boxes and other 'junk' material. Each of the houses had been brightly painted and numbered by the children.

Case study

The teacher worked with a group of five reception class children. Before the activity began she had prepared some strips of card which corresponded to the heights of houses.

The session started with the children talking generally about the houses: their colours, their numbers, their positions (first, second, third ...) and so on. The teacher then encouraged the children to make various judgements (estimates) such as which of the houses were the tallest, widest, would have the most living space. Eventually the teacher posed the question: 'How can we measure how tall the houses are?' The children's answers indicate their previous experiences.

Andrew: Use hands, blocks ...
Simon: With paper.
Gary: A ruler.
Andrew: With a measure you pull out.
Simon: Yes, a tape – a measuring tape.
Aimee: My grampy has one.

The teacher was then ready to introduce the strips of card.
Teacher: Look, I've cut out these strips of card and mixed them all up. Each one is the same height as one of those houses. Right, Jamie, here's a job for you. See if you can find one of the cards that is the same height as house number 7. [*Jamie takes a card and matches it correctly to number 7 without saying anything.*] What do you think?

Andrew: No, Miss, it's past there.
Teacher: What do you think, Gary? (7.4)
Gary: Miss, it's the same size.
Teacher: Come and have a look, Andrew. Look right in the front.
Andrew: Hmm, it's the same size. [*He puts his hand along the top as a guide.*]
Teacher: O.K. If we write number 7 on this piece of card, you will know that it's the same height as house number 7.

The children spent some time matching and numbering all the strips. The teacher encouraged the children to judge which strip would match each house before actually comparing them side by side. During the measuring itself the need to place the strip at the appropriate base level becomes apparent.

Andrew: You're not holding it right. It's got to start at the bottom of the house!

Comments

As a follow-up to the activity the children spent a considerable amount of time measuring the length of each strip of card with the aid of Multilink cubes. Although there was a subtle change in the direction of measurement (*along* the strip rather than *up*) this did not seem to bother the children, who were quite happy to talk about lengths of strips and heights of buildings.

While the children carried out this work the teacher was able to work with another group. When she rejoined the children they reported their findings.

Simon: Number 7 is fourteen cubes tall.
Aimee: Number 5 is eighteen cubes tall.

The children were then able to engage in some comparisons by matching and counting the Multilink cubes.

Aimee: Number 5 is taller than Number 7 by four cubes.

This produced a lot of useful number work and comparative language before the teacher decided to draw the session to a close.

Teacher: Before we finish, can you tell me which house you would like to live in?
All: Number 5.
Teacher: Why is that?
Andrew: Because it's the biggest!
Simon: No, the tallest.

Gary: It's the widest as well ...
Aimee: ... and the fattest!

Modifications and extensions

- Measure the widths and depths of the houses using Multilink or some other suitable unit.
- Measure the amount of floor space by covering surfaces with some suitable material (plastic squares if possible, but sheets of paper would do).
- Measure the amount of space (volume) in each house by filling with suitable material (possibly some building blocks).
- These ideas can be adapted to various other themes using a variety of non-standard units.

Shape and Space

Attainment Target 10 – Pupils should recognise and use the properties of two-dimensional and three-dimensional shapes

3-D Shapes	page 93
Shape Sorter 1	95
Shape Sorter 2	96
Capture a Shape	97
Geoboards	100

Attainment Target 11 – Pupils should recognise location and use transformations in the study of space

Polyominoes	page 102
Stars	104
How Shapes Grow	106

3-D Shapes

- You will need a selection of three-dimensional shapes. Provide cubes, cuboids, cylinders, spheres and cones in various sizes. As well as commercially produced material, cardboard boxes and packing can be used. Try to obtain some unusual shapes such as a Toblerone box (triangular-based prism) or a hexagonal powder box.
- Encourage the children to talk about the shapes, identifying and counting faces, edges, and vertices (corners). How do the shapes feel? Which are big and which are small? (What is meant by big and small?) What can the children make with the shapes?

Case study

Four 5-years-olds discussed a collection of three-dimensional wooden blocks with their teacher. This discussion had been initiated by some free play in which the children were building with their blocks.

The teacher noticed that Debbie was having problems attempting to balance a cuboid on the curved surface of a cylinder.

Teacher: Can you build on that cylinder, Debbie?
Debbie: No.

Rachel: The blocks keep sliding off.

Debbie [*turning the cylinder so that it stands upright on its circular base*]*:* I can build now, on its flat top.

Jonathan: You can only build on the flat sides of a cylinder, otherwise they roll.

James: Cylinders have round sides.

Jonathan: I've got a cone. Cones look like ice-cream cornets upside down.

Debbie: Put the cone on my cylinder ... It looks like a tower.

James: I know – let's make a castle.

Teacher: How many towers will you need for your castle?

James: Four, one at each corner.

Teacher: What other shapes will you need?

Rachel [*indicating the cubes*]*:* We could use squares.

Teachers: Are they called 'squares'? [*The children look carefully at the blocks. They agree that each face is a square and that there are six faces. The teacher reminds them that it is a cube.*]

Rachel: It's like an Oxo.

Teacher: These other blocks are called cuboids. Who can tell me the difference between a cube and a cuboid?

Debbie: One is big and one is small. [*The cuboid is upright and consequently appears taller than the cube.*]

James: Tip it over and they'll be the same size.

Debbie: No, the cuboid will be wider then.

Comments

Notice how the teacher encouraged James to predict the number of towers he will need to make his castle. Perhaps the other children could have been drawn in at this point to share their views, or perhaps they might have been involved in determining the number of cylinders and cones necessary.

The teacher's next question was again designed to make the children think ahead, and provided some useful comparative work on cubes and cuboids. Following this discussion the children were left to build their castle, a task they completed as a group and with much enthusiasm.

Modifications and extensions

- Provide the children with work-cards showing simple models that can be made using two or more blocks (Figure 8.10).

a tower   a chimney   a bridge

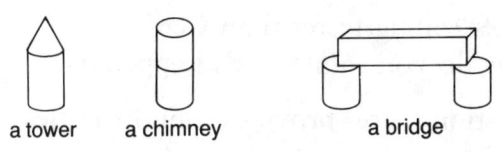

Figure 8.10

Challenge the children to build the models and name the blocks they use. How many blocks are needed to build two chimneys or one bridge and one tower? How many blocks to build a chimney twice as tall or a bridge twice as long? Can the children build a line of towers or a wall using repeating patterns of blocks? Encourage the children to set similar challenges for each other.

- Do some 'junk' modelling. This activity has links with art and craft.
- Make a collection of unusually shaped boxes and packages (encourage parents to help).
- Investigate nets of various cubes, cuboids and prisms.
- Using two A4 pieces of paper or card, construct cylinders by (i) rolling lengthwise and (ii) rolling widthwise. Which holds more? (Your sand-tray would prove a useful resource here. Alternatively provide rice or some similar filling.)
- Have each child take a turn feeling and describing a shape which has been placed inside a bag or under a cover. The remaining children must identify the shape from the description given.

Shape Sorter 1
- Provide a collection of three-dimensional shapes.
- Encourage the children to sort the shapes in a variety of ways.

Case study

This group decided to sort into blocks which rolled and blocks which did not. The teacher felt it would be useful to get the children to predict whether or not a shape would roll. Each child selected a block and said whether or not they thought it would roll. It was then placed on an incline and the hypothesis tested.

Ceri: Yes, it's rolling [*a short fat cylinder*] but it's slow; that's because it's fat, I think.
Dean: Mine's rolling [*a cuboid*]!
Peter: No, it's sliding – Ceri's went round and round – that's rolling. Yours is sliding!

Wayne: Mine's rolling faster than Ceri's.
Teacher: Why do you think that's happening?

The final question here provides opportunities for further investigation:

- Does the height or thickness of a cylinder affect its speed of rolling?
- How can we compare (or measure) speeds?
- What will happen if the steepness of the incline is changed?

Shape Sorter 2

- You will need a collection of plane shapes including circles, various quadrilaterals (squares, rectangles, trapezia), triangles (equilateral, isosceles and scalene), and regular and irregular pentagons and hexagons. Suitable sets are produced by the main educational suppliers in brightly coloured plastic.
- Allow the children to sort the sets in a variety of ways using hoops, sorting tracks (Figure 8.11), Venn diagrams and Carroll diagrams.

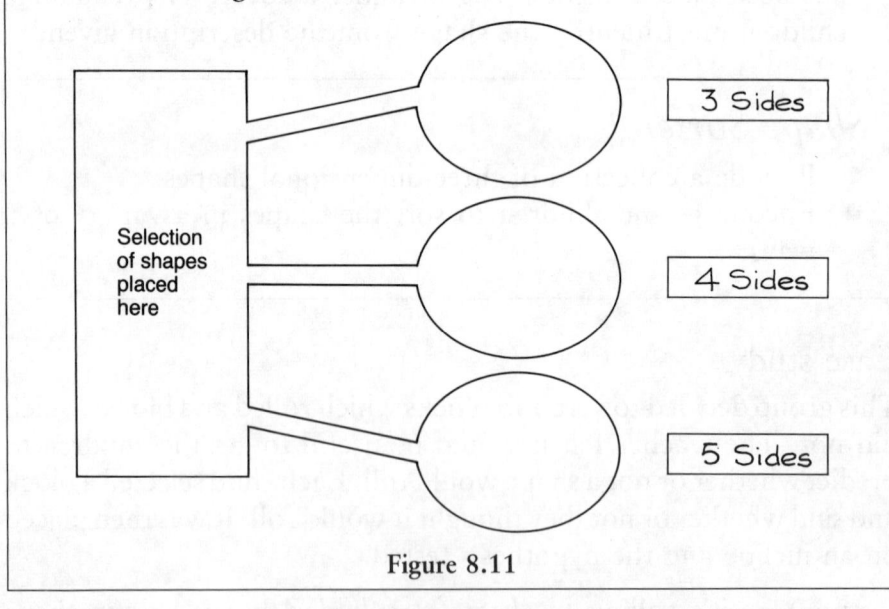

Figure 8.11

Case study

This group of five middle infants sorted a set of plane shapes which included semi- and quarter circles. They agreed to sort into subsets containing shapes which have three, four or five sides. Each child took a shape in turn and moved it along the track into the appropriate region.

Teacher: Who is going to begin sorting these shapes?
Kimberley: I'll go first. This is a square: it's got four sides. I'll put it here in the middle.
[*Ceri has picked up a quarter circle.*]
Ceri: This is a funny shape.
Teacher: Let's all look at the shape. How many sides has it got?
Lisa: I think it's two.
Hannah: There are two straight sides and one is round. That's three.
Teacher: Yes, there are two straight edges and one curved edge.
Kimberley: It's got three sides but it's not a triangle.
Karen: My turn. This shape has five sides.
Teacher: Does anyone know what we call a shape with five sides?

Modifications and extensions

- Have the children use the shapes to make patterns and pictures.
- The children could select two (or three) shapes and explore possible patterns.
- Use the shapes to make repeating patterns.
- Cover a given area with a particular shape. Encourage each child to estimate the area first, and then check differences between estimates and answer. Which shapes are best for covering surfaces?
- Explore which shapes tessellate, and sort accordingly.
- This activity provides opportunities for early work on fractions and discussion of 'half' and 'quarter'.

Capture a Shape

- Construct a board similar to the one in Figure 8.12. The number, types and colours of the shapes presented can be varied.
- You will also need an ordinary die numbered 1 to 6 and a collection of coloured counters for each child to identify 'captures'.
- Each child rolls the die in turn and captures (by placing a coloured counter on it) a shape which has the same number of sides as the score shown by the die.
- The child who captures the most shapes is the winner.

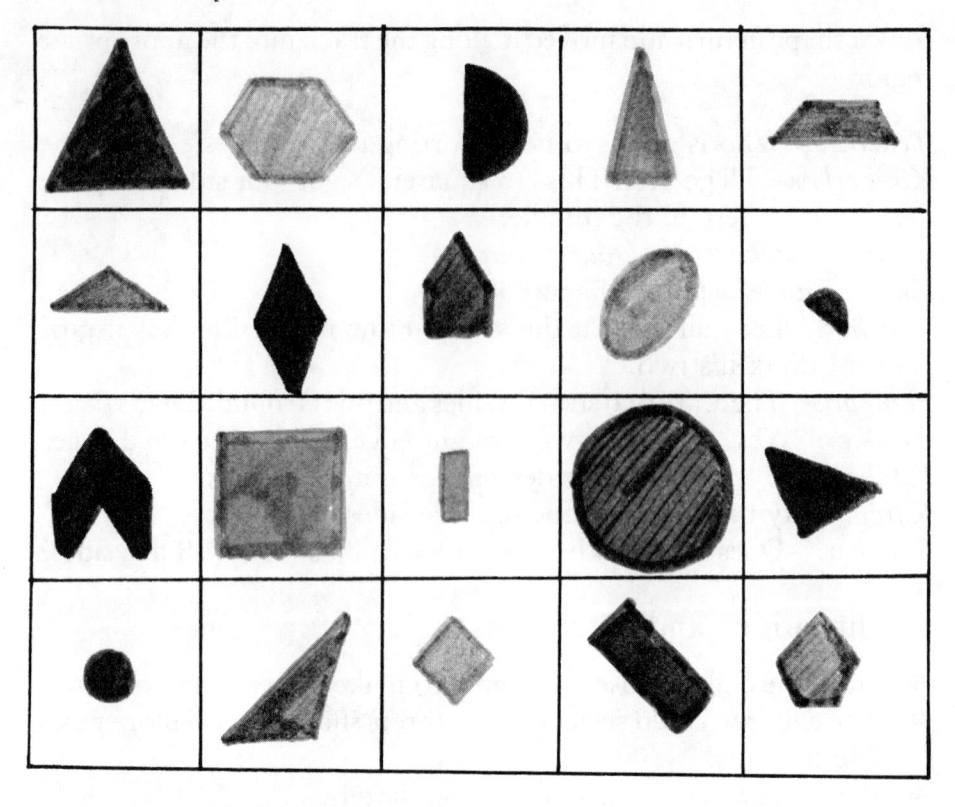

Figure 8.12

Case study

Four middle infants played the game, which is a Level 2 activity. Michael volunteered to begin.

Michael: Four – goody! I'll put mine on this square.
[*Rhia goes next and throws a two. She is unable to identify an appropriate shape.*]
Teacher: Oh well, perhaps someone else can help ... (7.4)
Jonathan: The circles haven't got any sides, Teacher.
Kimberley: Yes, they have – one side.
Teacher: Can you show us the side, please, Kimberley? [*Kimberley runs her finger around the perimeter of the large circle.*]
Rhia: I can see one with two sides now. [*She points to a semi-circle and counts*] ... One side [*the straight edge*], two sides [*the curved edge*]!

A little later in the game Kimberley threw a six. There was only one irregular six-sided shape left. She counted its sides and captured the hexagon without naming it.

Teacher: What shape is it?
Kimberley: A funny one like a bridge.

Michael: It's got a piece missing.
Rhia: It's like a pig's foot.
Teacher: How many sides has it got?
Kimberley: Six. ... It's a hexagon.
Teacher: What do you think, Rhia?
Rhia: It doesn't look like one.
Michael: It's because it's got six sides.
Teacher: Jonathan, do you think it's a hexagon?
Jonathan: Yes, it is.
[*A discussion then ensues as to who is actually winning.*]
Rhia: I'm winning 'cos I've only got four counters left.
Teacher: How can you be winning if they have got more counters?
(7.6)
Rhia: I've got more shapes so I've got less of these.
Teacher: Very good, Rhia.

The teacher was then able to leave this group to finish the game themselves.

Modifications and extensions

- The game itself can be modified in a variety of ways.
  - Reduce the number of shapes and/or the maximum number of sides included.
  - Restrict the game to straight-sided shapes.
  - Increase the number of sides and use two dice or a suitable spinner.
- Use an assortment of plastic shapes (one to six sides, regular and irregular) rather than a board. The shapes can be spread out on a table for the children to collect as they throw appropriate scores. It is always preferable to use concrete apparatus, if available, when introducing new ideas.
- *Shape Snap* This game requires a teacher-produced pack of cards containing illustrations of regular and irregular shapes with

a varying number of sides. 'Snap' occurs when shapes with the same number of sides appears.
- *Shape Bingo* Provide bingo-type boards on which are drawn a selection of shapes. Children draw a plastic shape from a bag in turn and claim it for their board if it matches; otherwise it is replaced in the bag.
- *Make a Triangle* The children are given an assortment of strips of card cut to various lengths – 10 cm, 15 cm, 20 cm, 25 cm, 30 cm, 35 cm – and split pins, and asked to make a triangle.

Ask, 'How many strips do you need?' 'Can you always make a triangle with three strips of card? . . . When can't you make one?'

The children can progress to making quadrilaterals with strips of card. Ask, 'Why do triangles become rigid when you fix them, whereas quadrilaterals are movable?'

Geoboards

- You will need geoboards and a collection of elastic bands. If geoboards are not readily available then the children could use isometric or squared paper and draw their shapes.
- Each child is provided with a geoboard and an elastic band and asked to make a two-dimensional shape.

Case study

This group consisted of five middle infants. The children had used geoboards previously to make their own pictures.

Teacher: I want you to make a three-sided shape on your board.
Craig: I know, that's a triangle – I can do it.
Cristian: I've made one – it's bigger than yours, Craig.
[*There is plenty of activity and talk as each child completes the task.*]
Teacher: Let's have a look at all the different triangles we have made. (7.5)
Claire: Some are big, some are little.
Cristian: Mine's upside down.
Teacher: Good. What's different about Craig's triangle? [*The sides of Craig's triangle all appear equal.*]
Claire: I know, Miss – the sides all look the same.
Teacher: Yes, the sides are the same length. . . . Now I want you to make a four-sided shape. What do we call a four-sided shape?

Cristian: A square. I've made one – look.
Michael: Mine's four sides but it's an oblong. Now I've made a diamond.
Teacher: Why has Cristian called his a square?
Cristian: Um, mine's a square: it's got four sides.
Teacher: What can you tell me about your four sides?
Cristian: They are the same.
Teacher: The same length ... Let's measure them to check.
Leanne: I've made a standing up oblong. Michael's is lying down.
Teacher: Let's look at Michael's shape. Is it a square?
Michael: It sort of looks like a square standing on its pointy bit.
Teacher: Yes, it's a square standing on a corner. ... Now I want you to make a five-sided shape – a pentagon.
Cristian: That sounds like pentominoes. We were making them with Multilink. Five Multilink to make a pentomino and now a five-sided shape ... Ha ha, it's good fun!

Modifications and extensions

- As a preliminary, encourage children to make and describe their own pictures on the geoboard.
- As a follow-up ask the children to make their own shapes using triangles, squares and rectangles. When the above group of children were asked to do this the following examples were given.

Cristian: I made a big square outside, then lots of squares getting smaller and smaller down to the middle, and a very little square [*Figure 8.13a*].

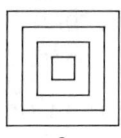

a

Craig: A big square outside and four little squares inside, all the same size [*Figure 8.13b*].

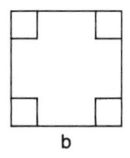

b

Leanne: A square and a triangle – two shapes, Miss [*Figure 8.13c*].

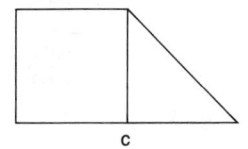

c

Michael: Miss, a big oblong with a little oblong inside it and a triangle on top [*Figure 8.13d*].

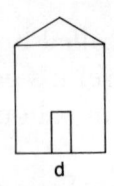

d

Claire: I can see two little triangles and two four-sided shapes and they're all in a big triangle [*Figure 8.13e*].

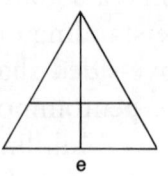

e

In both of these activities encourage the children to describe what they see in each other's pictures also.

- Draw a chalk line on the geoboard to act as an axis of symmetry. The children can use bands to make symmetrical pictures or to complete the other half of a shape begun by a partner.

Polyominoes

- Provide squared paper and coloured pencils or crayons.
- Challenge the children to find as many different shapes as possible by colouring adjacent whole squares. Start with two squares, then three, then four, then five, ...

- During discussion focus attention on what might be understood by 'different'. There should be plenty of opportunities to discuss ideas associated with:
  - *rotation*: How are

    and

    the same?

- *reflection*: What about

   and

   ?

   (Should 'flip-overs' be allowed? If so, the children could cut out their shapes to compare them.)
- *angle, position and symmetry*: What symmetries does

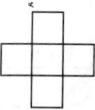

   possess? What about

   ?

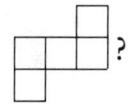

   Where are the lines of symmetry? What about the centre of rotation?
- This type of activity can easily become self-supporting if it is turned into a game. Each player takes a turn to draw a different shape on a large sheet of squared paper. As each shape is drawn the player is required to say why it is different from the other shapes already produced, or to make a statement about its symmetries. The other children should check and confirm that the shape is different.

   A variant of this is for player A to draw any shape using (say) four squares. Player B then attempts to draw a similar shape using rotational or reflective symmetry. It is then player C's turn and the round continues until no further shapes can be found. Player B then begins a second round by drawing a new shape. At each stage the children should state the symmetry transformation that they are using: 'I am reflecting it in the horizontal line', 'I am rotating it through a right angle'.

Modifications and extensions

- Allow children to use different colour shading to increase the number of possibilities. Begin with two colours!
- Have a 'grab a group'-type activity in which player A grabs a handful of Unifix or Multilink blocks and places them on squared paper to produce a shape. Each cube must occupy a square so the shapes will remain 'flat'. Player B attempts to make a different

shape using the same number of blocks. The round continues until no new shapes can be found. Player B then begins a second round.
- Dispense with the squared paper and challenge the children to build three-dimensional shapes.
- Use blocks in two (or more) colours.
- Place emphasis on area by asking for shapes which cover (say) four squares (Figure 8.14).

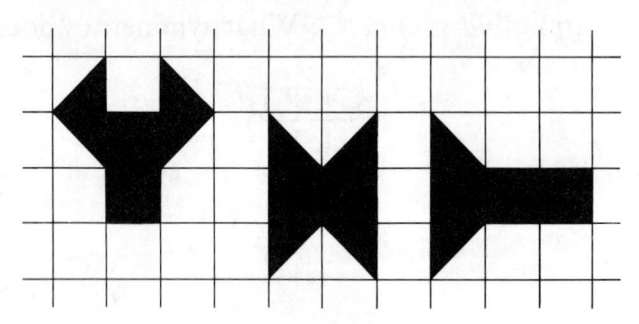

Figure 8.14

Stars
- You will need sets of two-dimensional shapes including triangles, quadrilaterals, pentagons and hexagons. Plastic shapes are best but if these are unavailable then you could make your own using card or stiff paper.
- Challenge the children to make some stars.

Case study
The teacher worked with a group of six middle infants. There were sufficient shapes for the children to work individually, but the children shared their ideas. Claire was the first to complete a star. She had used a pentagon and five triangles to produce what she called a 'pentagon star'.

James was the next to contribute.

James: If you put four squares together you get a 'window-star'.
Cara: It's not pointy enough, the corners are square. If you turn it around it looks more pointy. [*She rotates the 'star' to produce a diamond shape.*]
Laura: Now I've made a star. Mine's got one, two, three, four points.
Cara: I've made one using a hexagon and six triangles.

[*In the meantime James has been persevering with the squares and has produced an interesting variation.*]

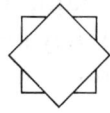

Teacher: Let's look at James's star. Can you tell us how you made that? (7.2)
James: You put one square down and then one on top and you turn it – it's got one, two, three, four, five, six, seven, eight points.
Laura: I can do the same with two diamonds!
Cara: Mine has got lots of points – one, two, three ... twelve!
Rachel: I can't make one from my shape [*a rectangle*].
Claire: Look. Two rectangles will make a square so you can do the same as James did.
Dale: Yes, and two fat triangles make a square so we could use those as well!

Comments

This simple activity produced a wealth of ideas, many of which could be exploited in follow-up sessions. Cara's observation that square corners are not suitable for stars could lead on to a sorting activity in which attention is focused on the notion of angle, and right angles in particular. James's clever rotation of one square on top of another opens the door for a further investigation. What if three (or more squares) are used in this way? Or what about using other shapes? Cara began this investigation using two hexagons but it could be extended to include all the shapes.

At the end of this discussion session the children drew around their shapes to produce stars which they then coloured.

Modifications and extensions

- Sort shapes into two sets: those which are suitable for making stars and those which are not. Link this activity with the idea of angle which can be demonstrated using two strips of card pinned together with a paper fastener. The arms of the model can be opened and closed to indicate angles of various size.
- Introduce the terms 'right angle' and 'straight angle' into your discussion. Investigate which shapes have angles that can be used to make a straight angle, such as two squares or three equilateral triangles. Sort shapes into sets according to this, and similar, criteria.

- Encourage the children to make stars by using one shape, such as a square. They could draw around their shape, rotate it, draw around it again, rotate it again, and so on.

    How many rotations can they include? How many points does their star have? How are the points related to the rotations?

    Use various shapes.
- Focus attention on one particular star. For example, using various combinations of red and yellow triangles, how many different stars can the children make (Figure 8.15)? Be prepared to help the children to negotiate their own interpretation of what might be considered 'the same'.

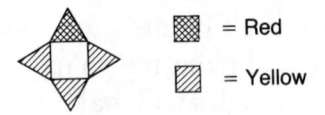

▦ = Red

▨ = Yellow

Figure 8.15

- Prepare a worksheet which shows a number of stars of a particular type (begin with the star shown in Figure 8.15). Have the children try to make as many different stars as possible using two colours only. Repeat for three colours and/or different stars.

    This activity could become a game in which each child attempts to produce a different star in turn. The child must say *how* it is different from previous stars to score a point.

How Shapes Grow

- This is an activity using Polydron triangles. Any collection of equally sized equilateral triangles could be used.

Case study

This group of five middle infants were experienced Polydron builders, capable of manipulating the material skilfully. Only triangles were available as the other shapes were already in use. The children set up their own problem.

Gareth: We've only got triangles.

Michelle: But we've got all the colours.

Luke: Let's make the biggest triangle in the world. [*This produces a reaction from David.*]

David: You can only make triangles with triangles.

Luke: No, you can make a pentagon with triangles.

David: How?

Luke: If you fix five together. [*He tries it and finds that six are needed.*]

David: That's not a pentagon, then.

Luke: No, but you can make a bigger triangle if you put a triangle – I mean three triangles – like this:

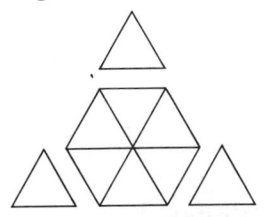

Michelle: We're supposed to make the biggest triangle in the world.

Teacher: How many triangles are you going to use for the next row?

David [*picking up a handful and fixing them one by one*]: One, two, three ... seven.

[*The children are surprised that by building on one row the size of the whole triangle is increased but the shape remains the same. They try adding another row onto a different edge and find that they have a further triangle.*]

Aimee: You don't get this with the squares.

Teacher: Now, before this triangle gets any bigger, try to estimate how many extra triangles you need.

David: You need the same and two more.

Teacher: Explain that again, David, and show us what you mean.

[*David counts out the seven triangles along one edge and places two extra pieces, one at each end. All the children agree.*]

Comments

Although this session began with some free-play shape activity, it developed into a very interesting piece of algebraic work in which the children were all able to recognise and understand the simple formula articulated by David, 'You need the same and two more'. This is a Level 4 skill; the earlier observation (see page 53) that children are able to attain at a variety of different levels within the same activity is thus reinforced. It was also interesting to note how Aimee was able to call on past experience and note that 'You don't get this with the squares'.

Modifications and extensions

- The children might consider the *total* number of triangles needed to produce their successive models.
- Investigate how squares grow.

- Use Multilink cubes and investigate how many are required to produce larger cubes.
- Construct a shape by shading in some squares on squared paper. How many squares need to be shaded to produce a similar shape twice as big, three times as big, etc.?

Handling Data

Attainment Target 12 – Pupils should collect, record and process data

Long, Short, Cream or White!	page 108
Record Cards	110

Attainment Target 13 – Pupils should represent and interpret data

Sorting and Classifying	page 113
Spots and Sneezes	114
Block Graphs, Bar Charts and Pictograms	116

Attainment Target 14 – Pupils should understand, estimate and calculate probabilities

Three in a Line	page 117
Jumping Beans	119

Long, Short, Cream or White!

- The emphasis in this activity is on allowing the children to decide for themselves what criteria to use when sorting and classifying a collection of objects.
- The activity had developed as part of a class theme on Doctors and Nurses. The objects used had been collected over a period of time and included various elastic bandages, surgical dressings and plasters. However, the activity can be adapted and used to support any theme.

Case study

This teacher worked with six middle infants who had considerable experience of sorting into sets. The children had recently used simple Carroll diagrams with structured sets of material, and this experience was evident as the session developed. The teacher introduced the activity in an 'open' way:

Teacher: I'd like you to do some sorting with these dressings from our hospital corner – It's up to you to choose how you will sort them.

[*Danielle decides that she will work with Larissa and the other children pair up also. They all start examining the dressings.*]

Robert [*to Richard*]*:* Let's do stretchy things! Look [*pulling a piece of crepe bandage*], this is stretchy.

Danielle: Do we have to draw circles?

Teacher: If you want to. (7.3)

Larissa [*to Danielle*]*:* No, let's draw a line instead.

[*She gets a long rule and the two girls assist each other in drawing a line down the centre of their paper. Richard and Robert follow suit. Their sorting is soon well under way. A crepe bandage and Tubigrip is on one side, whilst a white bandage, a material wipe, a triangular bandage and a waterproof plaster are on the other. The boys discuss where the fabric plaster they have picked up should go. Richard wants to place it with the other plaster, but Robert does not agree.*]

Robert: No, it's stretchy. Look [*pulling it*].

[*Meanwhile, Larissa and Danielle have begun to sort for long and short, while Jessica and Rhys have decided on cream and white. Larissa and Danielle take note.*]

Larissa [*to Danielle*]*:* This is cream [*pointing to a long piece of crepe bandage*] and this is white.

Danielle: Let's sort them again.

[*They start to regroup the 'long' dressings, placing the 'whites' at the top of the 'long' section and the 'creams' at the bottom.*]

Larissa [*Pointing to the 'short' dressings*]*:* Now these.

[*They follow the same procedure as they did with the long dressings but find a problem with the plasters which are neither cream nor white. Eventually they agree to place them in the centre of the section.*]

When everyone appeared to be satisfied, the children labelled their sets. The end results are shown in Figure 8.16.

Comments

Larissa and Danielle were obviously the leaders here. Their decision to use a Carroll-type representation influenced the others. Notice, however, that they in turn were influenced by Jessica and Rhys whose decision to sort into cream and white provided the stimulus for further work from the two girls. This is a good example of how group interaction can provide the opportunity for children to share and develop their own ideas more fully. The final representations show that Larissa and Danielle were ready and able to sort according to a variety of attributes.

110 *Resource pack*

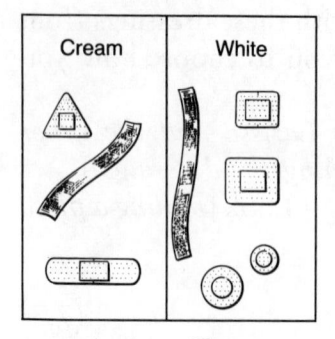

Jessica and Rhys

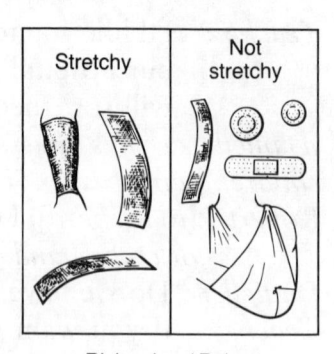

Richard and Robert

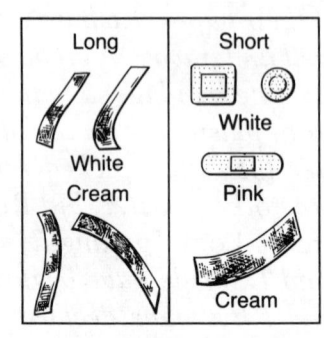

Larissa and Danielle

Figure 8.16

Modifications and extensions

- Adapt this 'open' approach to your class theme. Allow the children to decide upon their own criteria for sorting and encourage them to share their ideas.
- Introduce sorting activities requiring the use of two or more criteria and involving a variety of representations (Figure 8.17; see 'Sorting and Classifying', page 113)
- As children sort the objects, ensure that they describe them and justify why they are being placed in a particular region or being moved along a particular track.

Record Cards
- This activity provides children with the opportunity to collect and record information in an appropriate and systematic way.
- The data obtained can then be processed to obtain specific pieces of information or to create a database on a computer.

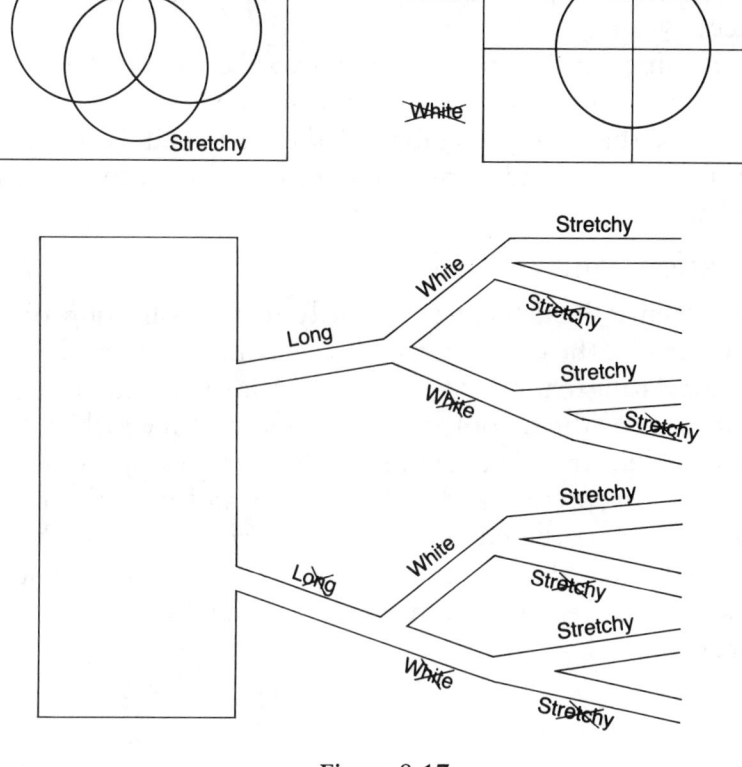

Figure 8.17

Case study

As an integral part of the Doctors and Nurses theme a class of middle infants attempted to build up a realistic set of medical cards. With the support of initial and ongoing class discussion and over a period of time, this was painstakingly achieved. The work involved:

- the cooperation of parents who provided information regarding place of birth, previous illnesses, and allergies;
- a great deal of general observation and discussion to determine attributes such as hair colour, eye colour, and sex; and
- considerable practical experience, with the children engaging in extensive measuring and weighing activities.

During the development of the record cards various groups of children took responsibility for collecting particular sets of data. One group decided that they would collect information regarding hair colour. Initially they headed two separate sheets of paper 'Fair' and 'Brown'. They then began to question each child in turn: 'Have you got fair hair or brown hair?' As a result of answers received, and due to various objections raised by class members, the number of headings (and pieces of paper!) grew to five – fair, brown, blonde, ginger and black!

After carrying out the survey (which involved writing the names of individual children on an appropriate sheet of paper) the group were able to check that every member of the class had been included (thirty-three in total) and transfer the information onto each child's medical card.

Modifications and extensions

- Many themes lend themselves easily to the collection of data. Alternatively, the children could be encouraged to gather information relating to topics of more specific interest such as the colour of cars passing the school gate, or the months in which children's birthdays fall. In either case allow children to be part of the decision-making process and to discuss how and when the information should be gathered, and for what purposes it might be used.
- The method of data collection used by the children could be refined by placing all of the 'headings' on one sheet and producing a frequency table.

Fair	++++ ++++ /	11
Brown	++++ ++++ ///	13
Blonde	++++ /	6
Ginger	//	2
Black	/	1

- As an extension of the work on 'Record Cards' the children discussed other ways of storing information. Some of the children had seen computers in their doctor's surgery so this provided an appropriate stimulus to the use of a database.

  The children agreed to enter information into a database under the headings Sex, Age, Height, Weight, Eyes (colour), Hair (colour). Since the data had already been gathered, and was available on record cards, each child was able to enter their own details. The majority of the children managed remarkably well with this transfer from card to computer file, and those that needed help found support from within their group.

  Once the information was stored, the children were encouraged to view the data and to interrogate the database. Initially the children were only able to suggest one criterion for data retrieval ('Let's see all the children with blue eyes'), but with experience were able to use two or more criteria.

Sorting and Classifying

- Children should be allowed to sort and classify a variety of unstructured and structured materials (attribute blocks, logic-people, etc.). Encourage children to decide upon their own criteria for sorting (see 'Shape Sorter 1' and 'Shape Sorter 2', pages 95 and 96), and ensure that they share their ideas.
- Introduce the children to a variety of diagrams and representations that can be used when sorting. For example, the following are easily produced using large sheets of card.

Venn diagrams

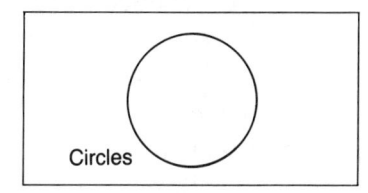

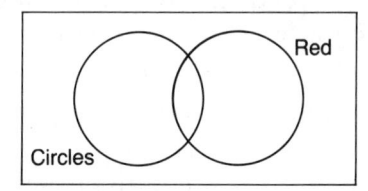

Carroll diagrams

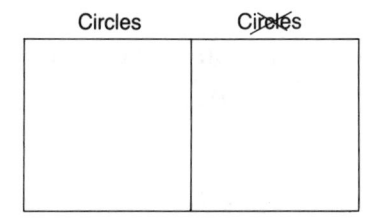

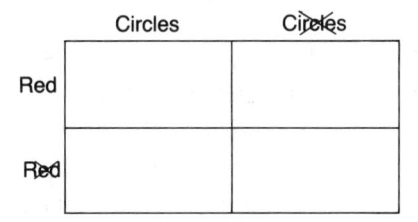

(The notation C̶i̶r̶c̶l̶e̶s̶ indicates that circles are not allowed.)

Sorting tracks

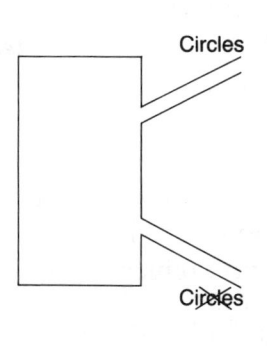

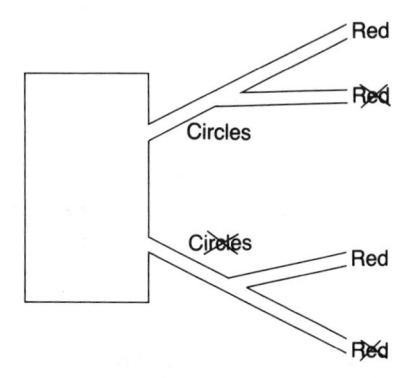

- As the children sort they should explain what they are doing and why an object is placed in a particular region or moved along a particular track.

Spots and Sneezes

- This activity is another that was developed during theme work on Doctors and Nurses.
- The intention is to encourage the group to use diagrams to represent the result of classifying using two different criteria (a Level 2 skill).

Case study

The group consisted of six middle infants. The children began by discussing various reasons for visiting the doctor. Following this, each child chose two different reasons and illustrated them by drawing and colouring a separate picture for each one. While the children were occupied with this, the teacher was able to attend to another group. When the teacher rejoined the children she brought with her a large sheet of sugar paper which had been ruled down the centre, and some small pieces of card to use as labels.

Teacher: What lovely drawings! Shall we try some sorting activities with them? How shall we sort them? (7.3)

Michael: The ones with spots.

Teacher: Oh yes, we can sort for the ones that have a rash and those that don't. [*Writes 'rash' on one small card and 'rash' on another (the children are familiar with this form of labelling) and places the cards on the sugar paper, one either side of the ruled line. The children take turns describing their pictures and sorting them into two sets. When they have completed the task the teacher summarises their work and sets a new challenge.*] That's fine. I can see that all the rashes are on this side [*pointing to the left*] and all the other reasons for visiting the doctor are on this side [*the right*]. What if we try a different way of sorting this time? I'll choose now – we'll sort for all the illnesses that are infectious. Do you remember what that means?

Ryan: You can catch them.

Teacher: Good. Perhaps you can each take your drawings back while I change the labels – 'infectious' [*writing the word on a card and placing it at the top*] and 'not infectious'.

[*The children begin to sort immediately. All goes well until ...*]

Gemma: That's wrong. You've got spots so it should go there [*pointing to 'infectious'*].

Rhia: No, it shouldn't. You can't catch eczema — can you, Miss?

Teacher: That's right, Rhia.

Rhia: I know, 'cos I've got it!

[*The children continue until the sorting is complete.*]

Teacher: Good, but I want to make it a little more exciting. I want us to sort for rashes and no rashes at the same time as we are sorting for infectious illnesses and things that are not infectious. [*She takes a ruler and draws a line horizontally across the middle of the paper. The labels are then placed with 'infectious' and 'infectious' on either side of the vertical line, and 'rash' and 'rash' on either side of the horizontal line.*] Who would like to go first?

[*Ryan volunteers, and picks up a drawing depicting himself with measles. He holds it over the left-hand side and after a short pause he places it in the top left-hand corner.*]

Teacher: Why have you put it there? (7.6)

Ryan: Um – you can catch it ... so it goes over here and I thought it should go in the top.

Teacher: Can anyone explain why it should go at the top?

Gemma: Rashes go up the top.

Teacher: Yes, measles are infectious so it goes on the left, and you have a rash so it goes at the top. Now, Gemma, show us one of your drawings, tell us why you were going to the doctors, and explain where you should put the drawing. [*Gemma explains that her drawing shows the time she visited the doctor with a sore throat. She did not have a rash and it was not infectious and so 'it should be put on the right and down the bottom'.*]

Each child then took a turn talking about their pictures, placing them in an appropriate region and justifying their decision.

Modifications and extensions

- Adapt to suit your own theme or circumstances as described in 'Long, Short, Cream or White!' (page 108).

Block Graphs, Bar Charts and Pictograms

- Use the data collected during your theme or topic work (see 'Record Cards', page 110) to construct and interpret appropriate graphs.
- For example, using the data that was collected when observing hair colour of a class of middle infants (see page 111) we might produce a block graph by:

    - Getting the whole class to stand in lines according to the colour of their hair
    - Using one piece of Multilink per child to build towers showing the number of children in each category
    - Sticking squares of coloured paper (one per child and different colours to represent different hair) onto card to produce a wall chart showing the number of children in each category
    - Using squared paper and colouring one square per child according to hair colour
    - Using the graphics facility of a database

- In each case encourage the children to:

    - discuss the graphs ensuring that the idea that one Multilink cube (or one square) represents one child is clearly understood, and
    - compare the number of children in each category, developing language (more than, less than, difference) and consolidating number work.

Modifications and extensions

- Construct and interpret bar charts in which a continuous column is used to represent the number of children in each category.
- Create and interpret pictograms where the symbol used represents a number of units (Figure 8.18).

Fair
Brown
Blonde
Ginger
Black

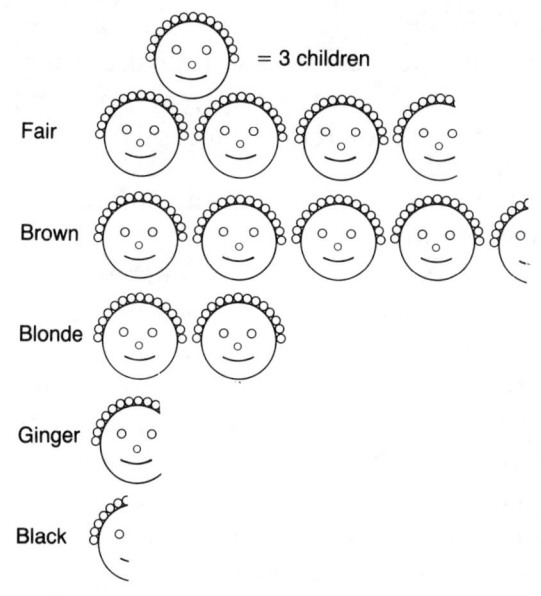

= 3 children

Figure 8.18 Much discussion and a variety of experience will be necessary to enable children to appreciate that one whole symbol represents (say) three children, and that part symbols represent two or one.

Three in a Line

- You will need a set of nine cards numbered 2 to 10 (teacher-made or selected from one suit of an ordinary pack of cards) and two ordinary dice (one red and one white) numbered 1 to 6.
- The cards are placed face up in three rows of three.
- Each child takes a turn rolling the dice and totalling the numbers obtained. The corresponding card (if available) is then turned face down.
- The child turning over a card which completes a line of three (across, down or diagonally) wins a point.
- All cards are then turned face up and a new round begins.
- The game is played over a number of rounds and the child with the most points is the winner.

Case study

The game had been played over a number of rounds by this group of top infants. They had noticed that certain numbers occur more frequently than others. For example, Michael had commented, 'That's the first 2 we've had' while Zoe had noted that 'We haven't had many threes or fours. It's nearly always 6, 7, 8 or 9'.

After the game finished the teacher encouraged the children to reflect on what had happened. The resulting discussion indicates that these young children had a growing awareness of some quite sophisticated (Levels 5 and 6) probability concepts.

Teacher: What can you tell me about the numbers that you turned over most often?
Michael: We had lots of sevens and eights and sometimes nines.
Zoe: We didn't have that many nines – we had more sixes.
John: We didn't get many twos or threes.
Teacher: I wonder if you can tell me why you think that you had lots of sevens and eights but not many twos or threes ... Perhaps it would help if you examined the different ways you can make each number on the cards.
Michael [*taking some paper and writing '1'*]: You can't make 1, so I'll put 'no' by the side of it.
Zoe: Put 2 down next. [*She studies the dice.*] You can only make it with 1 and 1. Now 3 ...
Michael: You can only make that with 1 and 2. Now 4 ...
Teacher: Very good so far, but wait a moment. Did you say that there was only one way to make 3? If I roll the red die and get a 1 and then the white die and get a 2, what will that make? ... Now what will it make if I get 2 with the red die and 1 with the white die? ... So is there only one way to make 3? (7.8)
Michael: There are two ways – 1 and 2 and 2 and 1.
Teacher: That's right, Michael. [*Using the dice to illustrate.*] The red die could show 2 and the white die 1 or the red die could show 1 and the white die 2. Do you think you can finish your list now? [*The children continue until they get to 9.*] Can't we make 8 with 7 and 1 also?
John: There isn't a 7 on the dice Miss.
Michael: You forgot this time, Miss [*they all laugh*] ...
[*The children complete their lists to 10.*]
Teacher: So can you tell me why you got more sevens than twos?
Zoe [*excitedly*]: I know – because there are six ways to get 7 and only one way to get 2.
Michael [*laughing*]: And no ways to get 1!

Modifications and extensions

- A simplified game could be devised using a single die and a set of cards numbered 1 to 6. In this case children should be encouraged

Discussion activities 119

to recognise the fact that each of the numbers on the die is equally likely to occur.
- As a follow-up activity the children could roll the dice a suitable number of times (perhaps 50 or 100) and record results on a data collection sheet.

$$
\begin{array}{lll}
2 & /// & 3 \\
3 & ++++\ / & 6 \\
4 & ++++\ \ //// & 9 \\
5 & ++++\ \ ++++\ /// & 13
\end{array}
$$

- Children could construct a block graph to illustrate the information.

Jumping Beans

- You will need nine dried butter beans sprayed (one side only) with red paint.
- The children take turns cupping the beans in their hands and rolling them onto the table.
- The number of red faces and the number of natural (white) faces are counted and recorded.

Case study

The teacher worked with a group of three young middle infants. To begin with they rolled the beans and noted the number of red and white faces showing.

Ceri: One, two, three, four, five ... Five white and four red.
Ben: This is like the four–five, five–four pattern. They always make 9.

After a while the children began to notice that some of the combinations appeared more frequently than others.

Ben: One, two, three, four, five white ... one, two, three, four red. Four and five. I've done the same as Ceri.
Daniel: That's odd. Ceri did four and five and I did four and five. It's like a pattern!

The teacher decided to exploit the situation further.

Teacher: This is very odd. How many different ways can we make nine? If they all landed on the red we would have ... ?
Ben: A set of nine.

Teacher: And?
All: Zero.
Teacher: If one turned over?
All: Eight and one ... Seven and two ... Six and three.
Teacher: If another turned over?
All: Five and four.
Ceri: Four and five.
All: Three and six ... Two and seven ... Eight and one.
Daniel: A white set.
Ceri: A set of nine whites.
Teacher: There were lots of ideas there, weren't there? Look at the paper. This has come up twice [*pointing to five white and four red beans*] and this has [*five red and four white beans*].
Ceri: I think this will come up twice [*pointing to the seven red, two white*].
Teacher: Don't you think it is strange that the same ones come up?
Ben: Every time.
Teacher: Do you think it would be an idea for us to see how many times each one comes up?

The teacher suggested that the children should roll the beans twenty times and make a record of the number of times each combination is realised. After further discussion the children agreed to record their outcomes in the form of a frequency table (Figure 8.19).

Comments

This activity, which was planned as a piece of consolidation work on number bonds and conservation, developed into a valuable piece of investigatory work. Having completed the frequency table the children were keen to discuss their findings.

Ceri: We haven't had nine and zero.
Daniel: Nor eight white and one red.
Ben: I don't believe this – there are lots of five–fours.

When asked if they could explain the results, the children had mixed ideas.

Ben: It's just the way you throw them. You don't know how many you're going to get. You can't fix it.
Ceri: You know you're going to get nine. But it could be nine red and no white, or eight red and one white.
Daniel: It's a lucky blow. If you did it on Snowdon the wind would blow them over. It would blow them all!

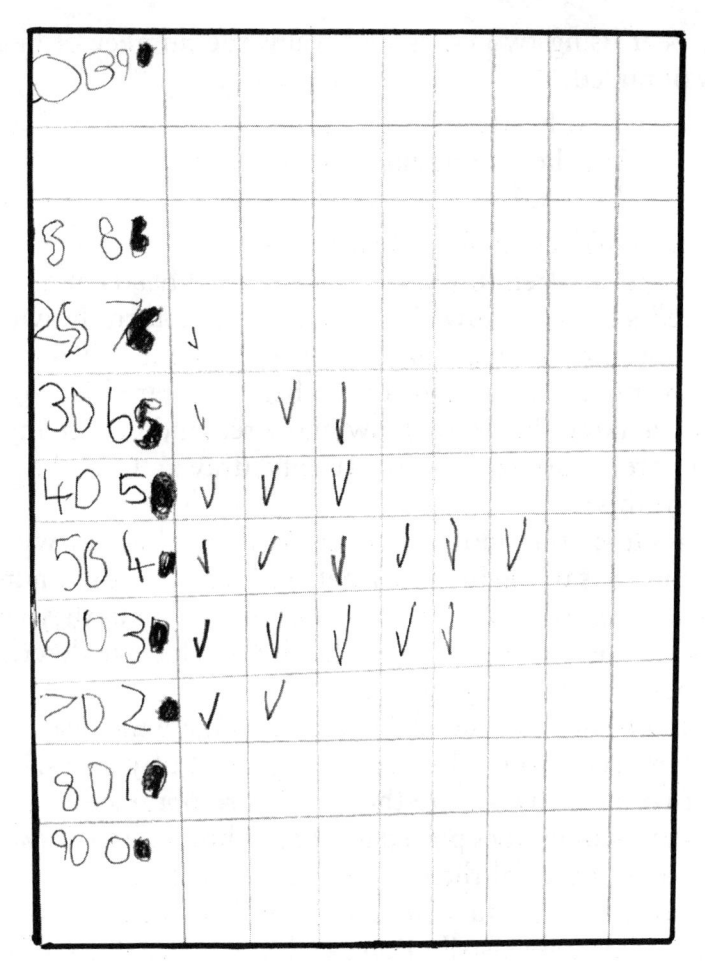

Figure 8.19

Modifications and extensions
- Use coins instead of beans. The children count and record the number of heads and tails that occur. Alternatively, use centimetre cubes with three surfaces coloured red and three coloured white.
- Vary the number of beans or coins used.

   Begin with a single coin which is tossed (say) twenty times. This should produce a roughly even distribution of heads and tails. The children can construct a frequency table and draw a bar chart. Can they explain their results? What do they think might happen if the coin was tossed 100 times?

Repeat using two coins and count the number of heads and tails obtained.

Two heads	: ++++ /	6
One head, one tail:	++++ ++++	10
Two tails	: ////	4

Can the children explain their results?
- Allow the children to place some coloured beads in a bag – say two red and six yellow. Each child takes a turn drawing out a bead and noting its colour before replacing it. Encourage each child to predict the colour of the bead they are likely to obtain before making the draw. How many red and how many yellow beads are obtained in (say) twenty draws? Can the children explain this?
- A variant of the above is to present the children with a bag containing (say) eight beads but with an unknown number of reds and yellows. By making as many selections as they wish (but replacing the beads each time) the children have to determine the number of reds and yellows.
- Use an ordinary six-sided die and investigate the distribution of the numbers 1 to 6 when the die is rolled fifty times.
- Use two dice. Investigate the total score obtained.
- Use a set of dominoes placed in a bag. The children draw out two dominoes and total their scores before replacement.

Investigate the totals obtained over fifty draws – this does not result in the same distribution as with two dice. Can the children explain their results?

Bibliography

Ball, G. and Brissenden, T. H. F., *PrIME in Mid Glamorgan*, Mid Glamorgan Education Authority, 1986.
Brissenden, T. H. F., *Talking about Mathematics*, Basil Blackwell, 1988.
Burton, L., *Thinking Things Through*, Basil Blackwell, 1987.
Cockcroft, W. H. (Chairman), *Mathematics Counts: Report of the Committee of Inquiry into the Teaching of Mathematics in Schools*, HMSO, 1982.
Department of Education and Science, *Mathematics in the National Curriculum*, HMSO, 1989.
PrIME Group, *One Year of CAN*, School Curriculum Development Committee, 1987.
Shuard, H., *Primary Mathematics Today and Tomorrow*, Longman, 1986.

Index

'Across the River' 71–73
algebraic activities 74–86
angle and rotation 103, 105
'Arithmogons' 63–66
assessment 6, 8, 10, 23–24, 50
attainment targets 53, 54, 55, 74, 87, 93, 108

bar chart 116, 121
block graph 116, 119
'Block Graphs, Bar Charts and Pictograms' 116–117
'Boxes' 70–71
building ideas 61

calculators 65, 66, 70, 81, 85
'Capture a Shape' 97–100
Carroll diagrams 88, 96, 108–110, 113
cassette recordings 23, 24, 39
'Caterpillars' 74–75
checklists 23–24, 25
child as a mathematical thinker 3, 42
classroom organisation 14, 30, 32, 36, 49
closed situations 64
commercial schemes 14
communicative skills 5
communications breakdown 5, 14–15
common goal 15–17
conservation of number 7, 17–20, 120
conventional teaching 51
cross-curricular links 30
Cuisenaire 7, 12, 40, 89
curriculum development 38

data and data collection 112, 116, 119, 121
database work 110, 112, 116
data-handling activities 108–122

decision-making process 112
deflecting questions 49
Dienes 40
'Different Ways' 76–77
discussion-based approach 3, 5, 11, 20, 54
discussion
    as a teaching style 14
    importance of 3–7
    planning 28–37
    stages in the development of 30–32
doing and talking 3, 7, 28
domino activities 62, 77–79, 122
'Dominoes' 77–79
drawing out children's ideas 10–11, 22, 49, 50
encouraging mathematical discussion 9–10, 16
equaliser balance 60–61
Ergo computer program 81
estimating 56–57, 97
evaluating
    discussion activities 22–25, 27, 39, 53
    children's comments 9, 13, 43, 48

frequency table 112, 120, 121

games 32–36, 57, 61, 71, 106
'Geoboards' 100–102
generalisations 73, 78
'Grab a Group' 55–57, 103
group
    skills 5
    work 14, 28

holding back 48
home–school tasks 87
'Houses of Hamlyn' 90–92
'How Shapes Grow' 106–107

Index

ideal response 9, 13
Inset activities 38–44, 53
investigations 7, 34, 38, 59, 69, 72–73, 79, 80–81, 88, 96, 105–106, 107, 122
investigative work 5, 73

'Jumping Beans' 119–122

language
  development 3–5, 10, 12
  patterns 11, 51
  skills 21, 24
learning 3, 25, 51
levels of attainment 53, 55, 78, 87, 107, 118
logic people 113
'Long, Short, Cream or White!' 108–110

'Make an Orange' 89–90
'Make a Triangle' 100
'Make Fifteen' 82–84
management of resources 30, 36
measuring activities 87–92
MEP (Microelectronics Programme) 81
Micro Primer Pack 81
mismatch of perceptions 5, 15
Multilink 7, 12, 75, 91, 103, 107, 116

National Curriculum 3, 6, 53
negotiation
  of meaning 3, 34
  of understanding 15, 48, 53, 72
Nuffield Mathematics 60
number activities 4–5, 10–11, 16, 40–41, 55–73
'Number Dump' 58–59
'Number Frames' 79–81
number patterns 4–6, 32–36, 79–81

odd and even numbers 77
open-ended activities 47
open tasks 6–7, 108
organisation 28–31

pattern seeking 73
pattern work 12, 17–19, 32–36, 74–77, 97
  see also number patterns
personalising 20, 48

personal skills 3–5, 21, 24, 38
Piaget 3
pictograms 116
place value 65
Polydron 106
'Polyominoes' 102–104
positive attitudes 6
practical work 3, 22
predicting and testing 61, 72–73, 80, 94
PRIME (Primary Initiatives in Mathematics Education) 65, 66
problem solving 38, 72–73
probability
  activities 117–122
  distribution 121, 122

question-and-answer 9, 48, 50
questions
  challenging 22, 47
  closed 9, 13, 17, 38
  helpful 51, 69
  open 13, 17, 38
  redirecting 49
  searching 50

'Record Cards' 110–112
recording 5, 7, 36, 69, 70
reflection as part of the learning process 22–23, 24, 38, 118
reporting back 42
respect for children's ideas 6, 17, 20, 21, 48
responsibility for learning 3
role of the teacher 47–52, 53, 54

sampling activities for probability 122
Scottish Primary Mathematics Group 60
self supporting activities 32, 37, 39, 49, 69–70, 83, 89, 103
shape and space activities 93–107
'Shape Bingo' 100
'Shape Sorter 1' 95–96
'Shape Sorter 2' 96–97
sharing and comparing ideas 3, 5–6, 10, 15, 38, 49, 109
similar shapes 107
'Snap' activities 59, 62, 99–100
social skills 3–5, 10, 21
'Sorting and Classifying' 113

sorting sets 55–57, 77, 87, 95–97, 105, 108–110, 114–115
sorting tracks 113
sorting tray 10, 22, 57
'Spots and Sneezes' 114–115
staff development programme 38
standard assessment tasks 6
'Star Number 1' 67
'Star Number 2' 68
'Stars' 104–106
symmetry 64, 102–103
systematic talk 34, 37, 49

taking turns 5, 10, 15, 36, 49, 50
talk 8, 12, 36
   see also doing and talking
'Tall, Taller, Tallest' 87–88
teacher
   activities 8, 12, 20, 25, 37
   development 38
   intervention 17, 53

tessellation 97
testing predictions 61
themes 76, 90, 92, 108, 111–112, 114
'3-D Shapes' 93–95
'3, 5, 7' 69–70
'Three in a Line' 117–119
time to develop ideas 31, 47, 48
timetabling 28–30, 37
'Trio Tricks' 62–63

understanding 3, 5–6, 16, 20, 21, 38, 50
Unifix 34, 75, 103
'Using the Equaliser Balance' 60–61

Venn diagram 78, 88, 96, 113

'What's the Number?' 57–58